Trust Fundraising

Editor: Anthony Clay

SECOND EDITION

DIRECTORY OF SOCIAL CHANGE

In association with:

Institute of
Fundraising

The fundraising series
For all titles available in this series see:
www.dsc.org.uk/fundraisingseries

Published by
Directory of Social Change
24 Stephenson Way
London NW1 2DP
Tel: 08450 77 77 07; Fax: 020 7391 4804
email: publications@dsc.org.uk
www.dsc.org.uk
from whom further copies and a full publications catalogue are available.

Directory of Social Change Northern Office
Federation House, Hope Street, Liverpool L1 9BW
Policy & Research 0151 708 0136; email: research@dsc.org.uk

Directory of Social Change is a Registered Charity no. 800517

First published by Charities Aid Foundation 1999
Second edition 2011

ISBN 978 1 906294 51 9

British Library Cataloguing in Publication Data
A catalogue record for this book is available from the British Library

Cover design by Kate Bass
Original text design by Eugenie Dodd Typographics, London
Typeset by Keystroke, Wolverhampton
Printed and bound by Page Bros, Norwich

Contents

The Fundraising series

Charity fundraisers change the world by raising the money needed to fund the tremendous good work that charities across the UK carry out day to day. Fundraising moves with the times and is constantly evolving. The economy, political landscape and trends in the way that people exchange information and communicate with each other all impact on the way in which charities ask for, and raise money. This makes the profession particularly dynamic and interesting. In order for fundraisers to be effective, it is vital that they are ahead of the game. Successful fundraisers identify future trends, anticipate demand and keep up with the latest techniques so that they can plan and develop appropriate strategies.

The Institute of Fundraising (IoF) and Directory of Social Change (DSC) fundraising series seeks to address the full range of fundraising activity and techniques in one series. Each successive volume seeks to address one key element in the spectrum of fundraising techniques. As fundraising techniques evolve and develop, new titles in the series are added to and old ones revised. The titles are intended as texts that encourage and debate fundraising within a professional framework – written and used by academics and practitioners alike. Each title seeks to explore the fundraising activity within its historical, ethical and theoretical context, relate it to current fundraising practice as well as guide future strategy.

The IoF is well placed to assist in the development and production of this series; without the support, assistance and expertise of its members and their colleagues, the series would not be possible. I thank all those who have contributed and continue to contribute to the most comprehensive fundraising series available today.

Louise Richards
Director of Policy and Campaigns
Institute of Fundraising

About the authors

Chris Carnie

Chris has been a fundraiser since 1980 and was a researcher in the House of Commons from 1982 to 1984. In 1990 he co-founded Factary, the leading European research consultancy. In 1993 he became the first fundraising researcher to be elected a Fellow of the Institute of Charity Fundraising Managers. He is Founder Chair of ICFM Researchers in Fundraising, a member of the Association of Professional Researchers for Advancement (US), and a member of the Asociación Professional de Fundraising (Spain). He is a trainer and presenter at conferences in Europe, including the International Fundraising Congress in the Netherlands.

He has written or contributed to four books on fundraising and research. Chris lives near Barcelona.

Anthony Clay

After working for 10 years as Head of Fundraising at the RSPB, Anthony Clay went on to spend another 11 years working in senior consultancy, helping more than 70 charities (many of them major nationals) with strategic planning and cost-effective fundraising, especially from trusts, major gifts and legacies.

Anthony has run fundraising courses for the IoF and DSC on 'Maximising the effects of your trust fundraising programme' and 'Developing corporate support and fundraising in a recession'. He has served as honorary treasurer and chair of the IoF (of which he is a certified fellow) and was chair of the institute's Professional Practice Committee. He was also chair of the institute's Working Party on the Code of Practice for Trust Fundraising.

He was a director of FR&C Ltd, the leading fundraising research and consultancy company, before 'retiring' in 2000 to set up his own fundraising company, ACC Ltd. He still does consultancy work, especially training, but spends more time on local voluntary work, as well as being a trustee of the Cambridgeshire Community Foundation.

Graham Collings

Graham has been a fundraiser for over 30 years, working with the Red Cross, British Trust for Conservation Volunteers and other charities in all parts of the voluntary sector. He has worked as a consultant, fundraiser and trainer with over 100 organisations, in campaigns large and small, and has been a tutor on IoF courses on trusts and other topics. He currently operates as an independent fundraising consultant and fundraiser, providing advice, practical help, mentoring and training. He works mainly with smaller charities, faith organisations and difficult causes, where trusts are often the mainstay of support.

Tim Finn

Tim is founder and managing director of the fundraising consultants Collyer Finn Ltd. He specialises in raising funds from the trusts sector. He works on behalf of charity clients, from the smallest to those of national size, in all parts of Britain.

Tim has contributed articles on fundraising issues to *Management Today*, *Debrett's People of Today* and several national newspapers. He has also written a regular column for *Professional Fundraising* magazine, and is an author of social histories, fiction and drama.

Peter Flory

Peter Flory is an independent information technology (IT) consultant, working solely in the voluntary sector.

He has been in the IT industry for more than 40 years, spending the first 15 years in a number of technical roles and the next 25 as a management consultant. He assists all types of non-profit-making organisations with the complete 'IT life-cycle' – from IT strategy development to requirements' specification and invitation-to-tender procedures, project management, quality assurance, implementation support and reviews of operational systems.

Peter also runs seminars on IT strategy and fundraising software and is a regular speaker on all manner of IT-related subjects for a variety of clients and functions.

Kay Holmes-Siedle

Kay joined the voluntary sector over 35 years ago as Head of Research at Charities Aid Foundation (CAF), where she was responsible for *Dimensions of the Voluntary Sector* and served as secretary to CAF's own grant-making trust.

Since then she has pioneered donor research in the voluntary sector, establishing a press library on individuals and a unique relational database holding information on the wealthy movers and shakers in the world of business, trust giving, professions and celebrities.

She has worked on some of the biggest campaigns in the voluntary sector at the NSPCC, Cambridge University, SS Great Britain, Woburn Safari and the National Trust.

She has also worked in partnership with many charities to establish their major donor, trust and legacy programmes, including UNICEF (United Nations Children's Fund), RSPCA (Royal Society for the Prevention of Cruelty to Animals), Friends of the Earth, Scope, CAFOD (Catholic Agency For Overseas Development), MAF (Mission Aviation Fellowship), RNLI (Royal National Lifeboat Institution), BHF (The British Heart Foundation), and many other smaller challenging causes.

Jay Kennedy

Jay is Head of Policy at DSC. He has worked for DSC since 2003; his previous roles included researching government funding for charities, project managing one of DSC's fundraising websites and being DSC's policy officer.

Prior to joining DSC Jay worked in the NHS, the National Assembly for Wales, a London housing association, local government in the US, academia, and advertising.

Adrian Longley

After almost 15 years' private practice as a solicitor, Adrian Longley spent the next 18 years of his life as legal adviser to the National Council for Voluntary Organisations (NCVO), where he sat on a number of working parties, including 'Malpractice in Fundraising for Charity' and 'Effectiveness and the Voluntary Sector'. In the 1970s he was a member of the Goodman Committee on Charity Law and Voluntary Organisations (which led, ultimately, to the Charities Acts of 1992 and 1993) and a UK contributor to Les Associations en Europe – Regime Juridique et Fiscal for the Juris Service in Lyon. An Honorary Fellow of the Institute of Charity Fundraising Managers (ICFM), Adrian is currently consultant to Arlingtons Sharmas Solicitors and has worked for many charities both large and small.

Roger Mitty

Roger has been a professional fundraiser for over 36 years. Having joined the charity Help the Aged in 1976, in 1979 he was seconded to several welfare organisations in South Africa, where he set up successful fund-raising operations for a number of causes, including a feeding scheme for township children and care facilities for the older black population in Cape Province.

In 1983 Roger was appointed head of Help the Aged's marketing group, with responsibility for the charity's income from direct mail, press appeals, Adopt a Granny sponsorship, legacies, trusts and foundations, and corporate sponsorships (the annual income from these sources at that time was around £10 million). His training in fundraising included visits to North America.

In 1986 he joined the Chapter One Group, a marketing and fund-raising services company, as Client Services Director. In December 1996 he helped to organise a management buy-out of the company, which led to the formation of FR&C Ltd, where he was a director, co-owner and practising consultant.

Redmond Mullin

Redmond Mullin is chair of Redmond Muffin Ltd. Formerly a Jesuit, he worked in research at Masius, advertising at J. Walter Thompson and fundraising with Wells, and has been a director at CAF where he was responsible for grantmaking and grant-making policy and for production of the *Directory of Grant-Making Trusts.*

He served on the board of the Family Welfare Association and on the Gulbenkian's Arts, Initiatives and Money Committee, and chaired the Advisory Committee for the Open University Voluntary Sector Management Programme. He has also chaired the IoF's Fellows Working Party. As well as being a trustee of the Dartington Summer Arts Foundation, Redmond managed a significant family trust in the West Midlands and advised Hambro Life (now Zurich Community Trust) on the management, structure and policy for its grant-making trusts. He has published, lectured and broadcast extensively on fundraising and related matters.

Des Palmer

Des Palmer worked for the Allied Dunbar Charitable Trust (now the Zurich Community Trust) from 1978 to 1996, where he was involved in a range of activities, including researching social issues (such as domestic violence, schizophrenia and dementia) and turning the findings into grant-making programmes, managing programmes, assessing applications and evaluating projects. He also wrote and spoke widely on fundraising for the smaller charity and on corporate community involvement.

He became a consultant, since retired, to grant-making trusts, giving advice to companies and charities on evaluation, fundraising and man-agement.

He wrote *Monitoring and Evaluation: A practical guide for grant-making trusts* and *Working Together: A practical guide to mergers and alternative options for crossroads schemes.*

David Saint

David Saint is chairman of Action Planning and is recognised as one of the not-for-profit sector's leading authorities on strategy, management and fundraising. A regular contributor to conferences, seminars, journals and reference books on the basis of his extensive experience, David has advised the boards and senior management teams of some of the most significant organisations in the sector, such as CAF and the Royal College of Nursing. He works closely with ACEVO (the Association of Chief Executives of Voluntary Organisations), delivering a number of its training modules for chief executives, and has been commissioned by leading funders such as Tudor Trust and Henry Smith's Charity to advise projects that they support with grant funding.

David is also very much at home working with smaller organisations, including schools, churches, and locally-based charities, and understands the challenges of managing small organisations with limited financial and human resources.

David established Action Planning in 1990 after working for 16 years in regional fundraising and fundraising director posts with Scope, Sense, SANE and Arthritis Care. He is a member of IoF (where he was the founder chair of the Consultants Group), a member of the Association of Fundraising Consultants and former chair of EU Consult, a European network of consultants.

David is a trustee of Andrews Charitable Trust, the Christian Initiative Trust and Advantage Africa, and a non-executive director of Andrews and Partners. He is an active member of St Andrews United Reformed Church, Cheam, where he has also served as an Elder and Church Secretary.

Anne Villemur
née Stephens, 1930–2010

Very sadly Anne died in February 2010. Before she died she very kindly agreed that her chapter on the history of the sector in *Trust Fundraising* should be included in the second edition.

Anne retired from CAF at the end of 1995, having first joined the foundation in 1980. She became editor of the *Directory of Grant-Making Trusts* in 1982, a task in which she was greatly helped by frequent attendance at seminars and interest groups organised by the administrators of major trusts. Thanks to the insight she acquired in this way, Anne was able to set up an annual series of workshops on the theme 'how to approach trusts'.

David Wickert

David has been Executive Director of Chapel & York Ltd since 1997. He is also currently a trustee of the ASDA [Wal-Mart] Foundation and a director of First Media Syndicate and the American Fund. He lives in Brighton. He specialises in advising charitable organisations and companies about the international financing of non-profit and media projects.

David was educated at King's College, London, ordained as an Episcopalian priest in 1966 and served in Wimbledon and Waterloo, London. He established the Waterloo Trust to work with single homeless people and co-founded the Upstream Theatre Club, producing plays in London and touring worldwide.

In 1986 David was appointed a director of CAF, where he launched tax free payroll giving (Give As You Earn) in the UK and set up CAFAmerica, an international grant-making foundation, in New York City, and served as its first director.

ACF (Association of Charitable Foundations)

ACF is the leading membership association for trusts and foundations in the UK with over 300 members ranging in size from small and local grant-makers to some of the world's largest foundations. Through its services to members it provides a framework in which trusts and foundations can learn from each others' experience, explore matters of common concern and achieve good practice in grantmaking.

Foreword

Anthony Clay

This is the second edition of *Trust Fundraising*, which was originally published in 1999 by ICFM/CAF as one of a series of fundraising titles. All the authors have updated their chapters to take account of changes in legislation and reflect modern fundraising techniques, especially use of the internet and the development of social networking sites. It focuses on a form of fundraising that could be described as following a virtuous cycle.

Grant-making trusts exist uniquely to give money away. They are also distinguished by a further set of characteristics:

- They provide highly tax-efficient methods of distributing philanthropy.

- Trustees share the decision-making process of where grant-making trusts' money should go; in other organisations this may be left in the hands of the philanthropist alone.

- Sometimes very experienced administrators are employed to examine projects, carry the burden of administrative matters, check on progress and – increasingly – seek out new areas in need of help.

- Fundraisers are frequently able to build understanding relationships with trustees and administrators.

- Grants can sometimes be made rapidly and effectively, often at relatively short notice, where companies may need longer lead times to develop programmes of support for charities.

- Above all, grant-making trusts provide around one-fifth of the total voluntary income of charities in this country.

For all these reasons, the benefits of grant-making trusts in terms of relieving human suffering, encouraging the arts and protecting the environment are enormous. However, perhaps because the cycle is so transparently virtuous, it has often not been paid the professional attention it deserves.

What information is currently available on grant-making trusts?

Many trusts (but by no means all) publish information about how much they grant, for what purpose, and their grant-making policies. Some also give examples of typical grants. Most of the larger ones now have websites which are usually extremely helpful to fundraisers in ensuring that applications reflect what the trusts are seeking to fund. There are other important publications for grantseekers and grantmakers available from DSC, which publishes a subscription database on about 4,400 trusts, and information about trusts in directories and guides.

IoF has prepared helpful handouts for its regular fundraising practitioner training courses in the fundraising series that it has been running with DSC.

Other organisations provide search facilities to enable fundraisers to focus on those trusts likely to be of most relevance to their causes (see Chapter 4). Fundraising research companies identify suitable trusts for their charity clients, sometimes using inside information that supplements the information in the published material. Fundraising consultants will assist the development of strategies for researching and approaching trusts. Several organisations provide training for fundraisers and volunteers on how to tap into this key source of income.

The original edition of this book was the first attempt to produce a publication that brings all these elements together in one volume, written by a range of contributors selected for their knowledge, experience and skills in each aspect of the subject. The new edition seeks to carry that work forward and bring it up to date.

Audience and aims

This book will be of value and interest to all who seek money from grant-making trusts, including private individuals, but the main audiences are trustees and employees of charities of all sizes. It is not, strictly speaking, a 'text book'; it is more of a compendium of the opinion and experience of a wide range of experienced authors. For those seeking a major treatise on the law relating to charitable trusts, Adrian Longley's chapter on 'The nature and structure of modern grant-making trusts in the UK' is an excellent introduction, but there is also much more to be read elsewhere. Those contemplating multi-million pound appeals should seek out the books available on how to win major gift campaigns, of which trust fundraising simply forms a part.

Fundraising has never been more competitive than now: the number of grant-seeking charities grows each year; state support for charities is declining; the demand for Lottery grant partnership funding continues unabated; many organisations that used not to be charities, such as NHS hospitals, are now hard at work seeking voluntary income. A book like this, that brings together the collective wisdom of so many experienced people, is indeed timely.

Much has been done by organisations such as the Association of Charitable Foundations (ACF) and the training courses from IoF, DSC and others, to raise standards of application and grantmaking. Regrettably, however, there remain far too many badly presented requests directed at overloaded trustees, seeking grants for irrelevant projects from trusts that are already fully committed.

The aim of this book is to help ensure that more of the right applications reach the right trusts, at the right time, for the right sums, for the right projects. This is no mean task for a single publication, but if this book achieves a small part of those objectives I hope that all its contributors will feel that their efforts have been worthwhile.

Structure

Part 1 provides an overview of grant-making trusts in terms of their history and structure. Anne Villemur writes a brief history of trusts. Adrian Longley presents the nature and structure of modern grant-making trusts from the legal point of view, setting the framework in which they must operate. Chris Carnie outlines the size of the sector and its relative importance in a fundraising strategy.

Part 2 concentrates on the centrality of research and planning in trust fundraising. Kay Holmes-Siedle writes on where to look and how to go about researching appropriate trusts. Redmond Mullin describes how to assemble a charity's funding needs into a coherent series of projects for support. Graham Collings completes this part of the book by addressing the question of how to plan each trust approach strategy.

Part 3 is given over to approaching grant-making trusts and considers the formal application, leaning on the practical advice provided by grant-makers themselves. Tim Finn describes how to make contact with each trust without breaking the rules, and Anthony Clay writes about making the application. Finally, Des Palmer presents the view from a former trust administrator.

In Part 4 David Saint deals with acknowledgement, recognition, reporting and keeping the trusts interested and involved. Roger Mitty writes on consolidating a trust fundraising campaign and Peter Flory outlines the computer systems needed, what can go wrong with them and how to avoid problems while creating an invaluable tool for the future.

Part 5 gives two different perspectives. ACF presents its advice to grantseekers on what, and what not, to do. David Wickert provides a chapter on US foundations, some of which may be particularly relevant to UK charities.

The final sections conclude the contributions, provide information about useful publications and organisations and supply a glossary.

Inevitably, not all our contributors agree on all aspects of the subject, but all that has been written reflects experienced and practical observations of what has worked in the past, and could be adapted for the future.

It will be evident that, being written by a number of authors, this book reflects different writing styles and several controversial ideas. Experience with the first edition indicated that few readers read it from cover to cover. Most found greatest value in dipping into it from time to time, especially when seeking a refresher course in a particular aspect of the subject. Because of this and because of the crucial importance of certain elements, we have allowed more repetition than would have seemed right in a publication which most readers would read chapter by chapter. So forgive us if you feel that you have read something before. This probably means that it is a very important point that another writer has also stressed, though usually in a slightly different context.

Acknowledgements

I am deeply grateful to all of the contributors and also to David Moncrieff of CAF and Professor Stephen Lee, formerly Director of ICFM, for inviting me to act as editor of the first edition and for their great help and guidance throughout the project, and to John Martin of DSC for all his help on the second edition. I am especially grateful to David Emerson, Chief Executive of ACF, for his many constructive comments and for granting permission to use ACF's excellent advice material. My thanks also go to the trust administrators who have commented on the work and responded to my cries for help. Nor must I forget my charity clients who have asked me to help them with their trust fundraising and have, in return, allowed me to learn practically all I know about the subject.

There are many others who deserve unreserved thanks, not least all the philanthropists who have so thoughtfully and generously set aside their wealth for the sake of others, and the innumerable trustees who give freely of their time to lead the trusts and award the grants. My very special personal thanks go to my friends and former fellow directors at FR&C Ltd, Kay Holmes-Siedle and Roger Mitty, who have lent their fullest support to the project and have, indeed, contributed two key chapters to it. Finally, I must thank my dear wife, Liz, who has for 45 years borne my late hours in the office with unfailing fortitude.

Anthony Clay

INTRODUCTION

Anthony Clay

What do we mean by trusts?

In the US charities are divided into two groups: *public charities* have multiple sources of income and exist mainly to carry out charitable work themselves; *foundations* are usually funded by one or, at most, a few benefactors and exist to give money away to good causes. Different rules apply to these two types of charitable organisation. Specifically, foundations are required by US law not only to distribute their income but also to give away 5% of their capital fund each year.

No such precise definitions or legal requirements about distributing capital apply in this country. All registered charities are treated in much the same way, whether they are grant receiving, grant-making, or both.

The words we use

The words 'trust' and 'foundation' are virtually synonymous and other words such as 'settlement' or 'charity' are in common use. All charitable foundations are trusts, i.e. they are managed by trustees who may, or may not, be supported by paid staff. A 'foundation' is a trust whose income derives from an endowment of land or invested capital. Not all foundations make grants; some use their income to finance charitable work of their own.

This book is not primarily concerned with charitable trusts such as those major national organisations that carry out their own programmes of work. It is concerned principally with trusts that have been set up by their founders as vehicles for the distribution of philanthropy, either for general charitable purposes or for the benefit of specific causes or groups of causes. Such trusts tend to fall into one of five groupings:

'Institutional' trusts

These are trusts that were set up several years ago with a number of trustees, such as the Wellcome Foundation. They make grants according to

1

very detailed procedures, making use of relevant professionals. Usually grant decisions are made at peer level so, typically, scientists present proposals for approval by other scientists.

'Private' trusts

Private trusts are often set up by one individual who takes most of the grant-making decisions on his or her own, or in discussion with a spouse. Such trusts are often set up primarily for reasons of tax efficiency.

'Family' trusts

These trusts are often set up by one individual, often in memory of an earlier family member or as a result of a discretionary form of will, with trustees who are usually related, or at least closely connected. Decisions are taken collectively but informally.

'Corporate' trusts

Corporate trusts are often set up when the income of the trust (and therefore its ability to make grants) is dependent upon the profits of a company or group of companies. Decisions will be made by directors of the company, increasingly now taking account of employees' views and interests. Alternatively the trustees may be largely independent of the company.

'Combination' trusts

These trusts are essentially a combination of one or more of the above groupings.

Such categorisation, though helpful in explaining the nature of the sector, can be misleading because few trusts fit neatly into one group, and trusts sometimes change from one group to another. Nevertheless, as will be seen later in the book, understanding of the structures, decision-making procedures, objectives and policies of each trust applied to is fundamental to successful trust fundraising.

Unfortunately, these important distinctions are rarely appreciated by grantseekers. Application is too often seen as a simple process, requiring only casual research of published directories followed by mass mailing of word-processed request letters.

An important revenue source

In 2009/10 there were around 9,000 grant-making trusts in the UK, with the largest 500 giving around £2.6 billion a year (DSC, 2010). This amount places trusts ahead of government spending, which is around £2.15 billion a year in total (*Government Funding Guide*, DSC, 2010) and is five times more than the estimated £500 million of cash donations by the top 500 companies making grants (DSC, 2010). So grant-making trusts are a very important revenue source indeed.

Trusts have great advantages as grant-making sources:

• They exist to give money away. Other sources such as companies and individuals do not.

• Grant-making decision-makers are often looking for new ideas and new directions. The modern pattern is for them to be seeking continually to be moving forward, so that past grant receivers do not become dependent on them.

• Towards the end of each of their financial years many trusts find themselves with money left over from previous allocations to projects that did not proceed. So it is quite often the case that grant money becomes available unexpectedly and at short notice.

• Most trust administrators are very experienced and keen to help charities to apply. The days when some administrators seemed to exist simply to say 'no' are largely past.

The place of trusts in a charity's fundraising strategy

Trust fundraising should not stand alone as a fundraising method. Essentially it should be part of an overall strategic plan, a key part of an overall approach in which the wider interests of the need to meet all of a charity's objectives are paramount. Sometimes this may mean holding back on a trust fundraising programme to prevent a relatively low-level application from preceding a much larger request.

A serious problem can arise when a charity is fundraising 'in boxes'. Typically, the fundraising department of a middle-sized or major charity will have a number of sections. These sections might include a corporate unit, a legacy unit, a special-events unit and a trust unit, each of which will have its own budget, targets or goals. Such a structure can lead to each unit becoming too possessive of its sectional interests. Ways have to be found to ensure that jealousies and self-interests do not get in the way of more important matters.

To whom should we listen: the grantmaker or the fundraiser?

The duty of the grantmaker is to ensure that his or her grants achieve the desired outcomes and deliver public benefit as effectively as possible.

The duty of the fundraiser is to secure as much money as possible for the cause, with complete honesty, while complying with the requirements of the law and following best practice.

The difference between the two is epitomised by the different answers given to the question: 'Should fundraisers go straight to the grantmaker's trustees, or to the administrator, grant secretary or correspondent?'

ACF advises quite clearly that the approach should be to the administrators, who are often appointed by the trustees for the very purpose of protecting them from the thousands of applications that are made each week.

The experienced fundraiser will say that it is crucial to seek to make contact with the trustees whenever possible. It is the trustees who make the final decisions, and there is a duty on fundraisers to go to the top – to the people who matter most. Of course, when making formal applications, the routes the grantmaker lays down should be followed. But imagine how more successful it would be if, at the vital moment of decision-making, a request is fully understood and endorsed by the majority of the trustees who know the project and some of the people involved with it. It is usually much easier for trustees to say 'no' to people they do not know than to people they do.

Unashamedly, this book sides with the fundraisers on this issue, in the hope that, when each side understands the other, the virtuous cycle occurs where trusts make major contributions to pioneering projects that make a significant difference to the fulfilment of important charitable objectives.

PART ONE

Grant-making Trusts

CHAPTER ONE

The historical context

Anne Villemur

A brief history of grant-making trusts

Grant-making trusts are not entirely an invention of the twentieth century. Of those listed in the *Directory of Grant-Making Trusts*, 160 were set up before 1900. Where did the idea stem from? On what base were the trusts built?

The financial underpinning of the earlier trusts is to be found in four main areas:

Religious and church property

These trusts range from the very large, such as the Trust for London, to a myriad of very small parochial funds, many of which have remained hidden for decades. Efforts have been made in various parts of the country to uncover these hidden pools of wealth.

Property (for example, land)

The oldest and largest of these, founded in 1626, is the Henry Smith's Charity, of which the assets include large swathes of Kensington.

Livery companies

Livery companies were originally set up in the City of London as guilds and regulators of their individual trades. Nowadays, while some retain a regulatory role and most promote their specific areas of expertise, many operate as charitable trusts. Their resources vary greatly and the area of benefit often shows a preference for London.

Bequests

Nowadays, charitable bequests contained in wills are likely to leave money to a named charity, because so many of the larger charities have gained the status of household names. In previous times, bequests tended to be made in perpetuity for specific purposes in a small geographical area. One example of the more unusual purposes was money left to 'provide red flannel once a year to the poorer children in the village'.

When judged by the amount of money they give away, trusts established before 1900 are relatively unimportant, accounting for only approximately 7% of the total grants listed in the *Directory of Grant-Making Trusts*.

Trusts in the twentieth century

Many important trusts were established in the early part of the last century, often motivated by religion. People who had built up large fortunes through successful commercial ventures felt that it was only right to share some of their wealth with the less fortunate. Quaker families, in particular, set up a number of important trusts. Such a sense of social conscience was not always the motivating factor, however; one large trust was created because the family of the settlor wanted to avoid swingeing 'death duties'.

From 1950 onwards the number of trusts set up each year increased dramatically. One of the reasons is that charities and charitable trusts had come under scrutiny: in 1952 the Nathan Committee on Charitable Trusts reported that, for trusts to be of maximum benefit to the community, it was essential to produce a means by which trusts could learn of each other's existence. This means came into being with the Charities Act 1960 which, among other things, established a Central Register of Charities, open to the public. Heightened public awareness of charity in general and the relationship of charitable trusts to charitable activity may have resulted in philanthropically minded people deciding to establish charitable trusts rather than make straight donations to the charities of their choice.

Inevitably, this increased knowledge exposed the trusts to publicity which some of their trustees would gladly have avoided. Not only were they exposed to public view on the Central Register at the Charity Commission in London but also, in 1968, the first edition of the *Directory of Grant-Making Trusts* was published.

At the time, most trustees felt that their trust was a private, family affair and that they were quite capable of deciding to whom grants should go. The concept of a partnership between grantmakers and grantseekers was something envisaged only by the more radically minded trusts.

Into the limelight

The first publication of the *Directory of Grant-Making Trusts* in 1968 represented a turning point. Shortly after publication, the publishers began to be the target of angry letters from trusts accusing them of causing a 'bombardment of applications' with which they could not cope. The privacy of trusts had been threatened. They were not impressed by the argument that, because their incomes were tax free, their decisions should be subject to public scrutiny. Some insisted that for subsequent editions their entries should include the admonition, 'no unsolicited applications will be considered by the trustees'.

This negative reaction is likely to have had something to do with the fact that the average board of trustees at that time was middle-aged and middle class. Even the salaried directors of the larger trusts were drawn from the ranks of the retired professional classes.

The American context

On the international scene, it is in the US that trusts and foundations have become most common. As may be expected from the fact that a great number of these trusts and foundations are based in commercial companies, they are extremely business-like. In the past American foundations associated with each other in a way that would not have been envisaged by their UK counterparts at the time. Currently their professional association, based at the Foundation Center in New York, has a large staff headed by a president who plays an important role in the life of US foundations. The Center publishes the comprehensive *Foundation Center Directory Online* – www.foundationcenter.org. It also provides help to grant-seeking bodies in the shape of workshops on how best to prepare an application (or 'proposal' as they are called in the US). For more on US grant-making trusts see Chapter 14, page 105.

Some say good ideas take a certain time to cross the Atlantic from west to east. Little by little, UK trusts began to get together to discuss their grantmaking. At first, this was an 'old boys' network' of directors of major trusts, but once the first step away from anonymity had been taken (with the Charities Act and the publication of the *Directory of Grant-Making Trusts*), things were bound to change. Trusts began to employ more and more paid staff, and assistant directors formed a loose association that met at residential seminars to which experts in the sociological field were invited to address delegates from a wide variety of trusts.

The current position

A new type of trust director began to emerge in the late 1980s. Many had a background of social work that made them naturally inclined to share information and opinions about the work their trustees were likely to find.

There is now in the UK ACF (founded in 1989), which gathers together a number of important trusts. ACF organises highly successful conferences and seminars and serves as a base for the meetings of various interest groups that study specific problems. It also comments on all aspects of grant-making procedures in its quarterly magazine *Trust and Foundation News*.

This togetherness sends a very positive signal to most grantseekers who, in the past, felt that the relationship between them and grantmakers was very much 'us and them'. Some fundraisers remain sceptical, and one is reported to have said: 'Applying to trusts is a game – and more like snakes and ladders than like chess.'

The community foundation movement

Since the early 1990s a remarkable development has been the growth of the community foundation concept. These are grant-making charities located across the UK, dedicated to strengthening local communities, creating opportunities and tackling issues of disadvantage and exclusion. Community foundations target grants that make a genuine difference to the lives of local people. They manage funds donated by individuals and organisations, building endowment and acting as a link between donors and local needs, connecting people with causes and enabling donors to achieve far more than they could ever do by themselves. They provide professional and personalised philanthropic advice and grant portfolio development for each client.

The Community Foundation Network, which represents the community foundation movement has grown rapidly over recent years. More than 95% of the population now live in the area of benefit of a community foundation. It is one of the largest independent funders of community organisations in the UK (making total grants of around £70 million a year).

References

Directory of Grant Making Trusts 2010/11, Alan French, Tom Traynor, John Smyth, Catriona Chronnell, Jessica Carver, Denise Lillya and Sarah Johnston, DSC, 2010

CHAPTER TWO

The nature and structure of grant-making trusts in the UK

Adrian Longley

Things and actions are what they are and the consequences of them will be what they will be; why then should we desire to be deceived?
Bishop Butler (1692–1752) *Fifteen Sermons*, No. 7

The trustees, who admitted to a lapse of judgement over the margarine, have suspended further endorsements until they draw up rules on what products are suitable. They have rejected requests for a Diana manure and rose-coloured carpets with her signature.
The Times, 25 April 1998

Introduction

Even if the trustees of the Diana, Princess of Wales Memorial Fund had weighed – or had weighed more carefully – Bishop Butler's famous admonition (contained, incidentally, in a sermon on the Old Testament prophet, Balaam, whose ass, it will be recalled, was more perceptive than her master), there is, of course, no guarantee that they would have acted otherwise and so escaped serious criticism and loss of public confidence. What, however, their confessed miscalculation indisputably illustrates is that in few areas of philanthropic endeavour is it more necessary than in that of grant-making trusts for those involved (actually or prospectively) in management and administration never to deceive themselves (or be deceived) about the potential consequences of their actions (or inactions).

What follows focuses primarily on charity law in practice in England and Wales. Slightly different systems operate in Scotland and Northern Ireland. A Memorandum of Undertaking between the Charity Commission and the Office of the Scottish Charity Register, published on the Commission's website on 21 October 2005, seeks to minimise the burden of regulation on charities operating across England, Wales and Scotland and to ensure joint consultation, collaboration and the sharing of information, as charity law develops.

A grant-making trust is one whose operations consist entirely of giving money or other forms of financial help to individuals or organisations for the fulfilment of their declared purposes. While such a trust is often set up as a charity – by reason of the perceived fiscal and other privileges which charities enjoy – it need not always be one; indeed, there can be circumstances where charity status is not in the best financial interests of the potential beneficiaries (see 'Charity status' below). Moreover, since charities are subject to constraints, including a supervisory regime maintained by the Charity Commission, promoters must from the outset be clear as to the permitted scope, direction and development of their intended activities. In particular, they must fully comprehend the nature (and limitations) of charity status, the duties and responsibilities of trustees, the constitutional forms available, the procedures for establishment and dissolution and, especially in this context, certain basic principles underlying trustees' policy decisions. Each of these important elements will be considered in turn.

Charity status

A brief reminder of the salient features will not be out of place. Fundamental is the fact that the legal and the Biblical or popular meanings of charity are by no means the same, though they may coincide. Thus, to the man or woman on the Clapham omnibus in 2010, 'charity' may still primarily suggest concern for those in need, hardship or distress. In practice, the range of purposes recognised by the law as charitable is extremely wide. Moreover, as Lord Hailsham emphasised in the House of Lords in 1980, 'the legal conception of charity (is) not static, but moving and changing'.

Accordingly, there is no neat, encapsulated definition. The Charities Act 1993, repeating an earlier Act of 1960, describes a charity as an institution established for 'charitable purposes'.

The Charities Act 2006 – the latest legislation in this field – states that a charitable purpose is one which falls within certain descriptions set out in Section 2 of the Act:

a. the prevention or relief of poverty

b. the advancement of education

c. the advancement of religion

d. the advancement of health or the saving of lives

e. the advancement of citizenship or community development

f. the advancement of the arts, culture, heritage or science

g. the advancement of amateur sport

h. the advancement of human rights, conflict resolution or reconciliation or the promotion of religious or racial harmony or equality and diversity

i. the advancement of environmental protection or improvement

j. the relief of those in need, by reason of youth, age, ill-health, disability, financial hardship, or other disadvantage

k. the advancement of animal welfare

l. the promotion of the efficiency of the armed forces of the Crown, or of the efficiency of the police, fire and rescue services or ambulance services.

However, these descriptions (or categories) are not exhaustive. Reflecting Lord Hailsham's 1980 judgment, the 2006 Act also confirms the inclusion of other purposes currently recognised as charitable and any new ones similar to another charitable purpose.

The time-honoured overriding requirement of public benefit is explicitly retained, but with a crucial difference. No longer, in the absence of evidence to the contrary, are charities established for the relief of poverty or the advancement of education or religion automatically presumed to pass the test. The trustees of any charity are now liable to be asked by the Charity Commission (itself placed under a statutory obligation to issue guidance in this area) to demonstrate, to the Commission's satisfaction, that their activities in fact benefit a sufficient section of the community, and in what manner.

Thus, even if the promoters of a grant-making trust initially have a restricted category of beneficiaries in mind, for example, the needy in a particular part of the world, it will generally be prudent to declare comprehensive objects along the following lines: 'To promote such objects as are now or may hereafter be deemed by law to be charitable', followed by a brief description of the restricted category. In this way, there will be no limit to the kind of charitable beneficiaries who may legitimately be supported, should the trustees' policy change over the years.

Sometimes, however, *any* charitable objects may in practice be inappropriate. For example, where considerable sums have been raised from a generous public in response to a (possibly over-emotional) disaster appeal the trustees of a trust established as a charity may well be precluded by the law from providing help that goes beyond the relief of genuine and immediate need. Any material enhancement of the victims' or their dependants' previous living standards can thus be unlawful, thereby presenting the trustees with problems over the distribution of surplus funds in their hands, unless the point has been specifically covered in the appeal and/or the constitution.

The trustees of a non-charitable grant-making trust are also far less likely than those of a charity to be embarrassed by endorsements of margarine, manure, matting or any other commercial product.

There is, of course, a crucial distinction between the objects of a charity and the means of achieving them. The former must be exclusively charitable in the strict legal sense. The latter need not – and indeed, by definition, cannot – be since they will include what are essentially commercial operations, from employing staff, providing pensions and investing funds to effecting insurance cover and acquiring and disposing of property. Clearly, in the case of a grant-making trust, the trustees' investment powers should be as wide as the law permits, and where substantial shareholdings are envisaged, legal ownership by a nominee company, along with reporting procedures and all necessary safeguards for the trustees (who remain ultimately personally accountable) should be specifically allowed in the constitution. Thus, trustees who allow surplus income to remain uninvested may be in breach of trust; while, having invested, they are under a duty to carry out regular reviews of their investments.

As to insurance, a distinction must be drawn between protecting the charity from loss and the trustees themselves from personal liability. Failure to insure will in some circumstances be inconsistent with the trustees' obligation to safeguard their charity's property. On the other hand, although trustees must not profit from their trust, an exception to this rule has been made in the latest legislation, allowing trustees to resort to their charity's assets for payment of premiums for personal indemnity insurance in respect of breaches of trust or duty, subject to exclusions such as the costs of an unsuccessful defence against criminal proceedings or conduct incontrovertibly reckless and not in the interests of the charity.

Unless specifically exempt or excepted by regulations, a charity should be registered with the Charity Commission. Registration neither confers charity status nor is an indication that the Commission approves or disapproves of a charity's activities or is satisfied that it has been or will be well managed. It is, however, proof for all practical purposes that the organisation is a charity at law; and some potential donors are explicitly prevented by their own terms of reference from supporting bodies which are not registered charities.

Duties and responsibilities of trustees

Trustees are people who hold property which they are legally bound to apply in all respects for the benefit of others.

Charity trustees are defined in Section 97 of the Charities Act 1993 as 'the persons having the general conduct and management of the administration of a charity'. They are neither required nor expected by the law to be omniscient. However, they must at all times act rationally, sensibly and carefully; they must take as much care in their business dealings on behalf of their charity as would prudent men and women over their own personal business matters. Not least, they must never allow their own personal views or prejudices to influence their conduct as trustees. Yet, *On Trust*, the 1992 report of a working party on trustee training, set up by NCVO and the Charity Commission, revealed that of those surveyed only one third actually realised they were charity trustees with strict obligations in law. Some charitable governing instruments, for example those in the form of an incorporated organisation (see 'Constitutional form' below) seldom mention the words 'trustee' or 'trustees' and this may help to explain, but not wholly to excuse, the prevailing ignorance.

Broadly speaking, those who are trustees must, in the words of the report *Effectiveness and the Voluntary Sector* (London, National Council for Voluntary Organisations, 1990), 'supervise the charity's operations and ensure that the strategic planning which guides those operations makes the best use of its actual and potential assets in meeting its defined aims. They are responsible for setting the targets, standards and working methods of the organisation and for being ready to modify these to meet changing circumstances'.

Charity trustees are collectively and individually responsible for all of their charity's activities. Although, in contrast to private trustees, charity trustees need not be unanimous, a dissenting minority will not escape responsibility unless they actively and publicly disassociate themselves from the relevant decision. Nor can the trustees, as a body, avoid ultimate responsibility by delegation to employees, agents or volunteers. However, a trustee who has acted prudently and within the scope of the charity's constitution will usually have the right to be indemnified out of the charity's assets. On the other hand, where a trustee's conduct has been negligent, reckless or outside the scope of the constitution, no indemnity will be allowed.

Constitutional form

Of the forms realistically available, choice for the promoters of a charitable grant-making trust lies in practice between a declaration of trust and incorporation as either a company limited by guarantee or a charitable incorporated organisation (CIO), the latter created by the Charities Act 2006 and regulated by procedures inserted into the 1993 Act. The structure of an unincorporated association, which frequently involves a membership wielding ultimate authority in general meeting, is not normally to be recommended in this context. Nor should a decision to set up a company limited by guarantee be lightly taken since it will involve compliance with both company and charity law. A CIO, however, is required to report only to the Charity Commission. Conversion from a charitable company limited by guarantee to a CIO is permitted in accordance with procedures in the 1993 Act. Both forms of incorporation postulate additional expense and a degree of sophistication on the part of the promoters.

Incorporation is widely seen as providing blanket limitation of trustees' personal liability, but this is a dangerous misconception. Incorporation may well afford the directors of a charitable company some initial protection against liability to the suppliers of goods and services. However, in practice, so far as ultimate personal liability is concerned, there may be little or no material difference between the position of the trustees of an unincorporated association or a declaration of trust on the one hand and that of the directors of a charitable company or CIO on the other. Undeniably, incorporation has attractions where the charity is likely to handle large sums and employ staff on a significant scale. But in the case of relatively small organisations, the bureaucratic requirements can outweigh the advantages.

On balance, a declaration of trust, which is relatively easy to establish and for which there are a number of useful precedents (acceptable to the Charity Commission) may often be the most appropriate in this context. Such trustees are almost always a self-appointed, self-perpetuating oligarchy not accountable to a participating membership.

Formation and dissolution

Where it is decided against charity status at the outset no particular problems normally arise – beyond ensuring that the constitution correctly expresses the aspirations of the promoters (i.e. those who are seeking to establish the charitable status) and lays down appropriate rules for management and administration – all within the general law. A special procedure, however, applies in the case of charities.

Until 1996, clearance of a draft constitution by the Charity Commission prior to completion of the formalities was invariably recommended. Today, unless circumstances are exceptional, for example when delay in formation could result in the loss of a substantial sum and the Commission is therefore willing to approve a draft provided full supporting information is supplied, promoters must first read the Commission's general guidance on the choice and preparation of a suitable constitution, the duties and responsibilities of trustees, the principles of public benefit, and applying for registration. It will also be prudent to study any particular guidance offered by the Commission in the light of its obligations under the Charities Act 2006, which appears to govern the promoters' intended operations. The promoters must then carry through the necessary formalities, for example, prepare, execute (and if necessary stamp) the constitution, complete a detailed application form (and questionnaire) for registration and sign a declaration to the effect that being fully aware of the organisation's objects and not in any way disqualified from trusteeship, they are willing to act as charity trustees, and that all the information supplied is true, complete and correct.

The application/questionnaire being submitted to the Charity Commission must be completed with extreme care; any casual or equivocal response can lead to probing by the Commission, with consequent delay in – and even, on occasion, denial of – registration. A crucial question relates to the trustees' intended activities, both short and long term. Thus, particularly in this context, the Commission will require to know how the organisation is to be financed and, if fundraising is contemplated, that the promoters are fully aware of the requirements and constraints in Part II of the Charities Act 1992 as amended by the 2006 Act. It will also need to be satisfied that adequate monitoring arrangements are in place or genuinely envisaged, including steps to be taken to ensure that all the beneficiaries' needs and/or activities are within the scope of the proposed charity's objects and that regular checks will be made as to the actual application of funds, not least where these are remitted abroad.

If all or some of the trustees are closely related, the Commission may suggest reconstitution to provide for a non-family majority; and while it has no power of enforcement in this respect, compliance may be prudent, and not only for bureaucratic reasons.

To minimise problems in the event of the Commission rejecting (or seeking to modify) the constitution, a wide power of amendment (not itself requiring the Commissioners' consent) should be specifically included.

Likewise, the constitution should specify the destination of funds in the event of dissolution – usually to some other charity or charities having objects similar to those of the trust.

Policy

All trusts are different, with individual interests and styles depending on their histories, policies and priorities – and, of course, the personalities and current predilections of the trustees.

However, there are elements of principle and practice which the trustees of all grant-making trusts should constantly observe, for example:

• While the trustees must bear in mind their trust's origin and ethos, they must not be impervious to organic change in the light of shifting social, economic and political conditions.

• A primary duty of the trustees under the law is to secure the best financial return on their investments. However, in certain circumstances ethical considerations may have to be taken into account – and a lower return accepted. For example, where a trust's declared object or principal activity in practice is the relief of sufferers from cancer or even the protection of health generally, the trustees must be extremely cautious over investing in a company promoting tobacco sales (not always easy to avoid in these days of conglomerates).

• The trustees should maintain a reserves policy – the process by which some of a charity's income is held for the future rather than spent or otherwise committed as it is received – appropriate for their trust's objects and the potential risks it faces. In its *Regulators Study, Charity Reserves* (RS3), published in 2003, the Charity Commission specifically recommended that grant-making bodies should not only publish their policies on grantgiving and towards applicants' reserves, but also develop grant application assessment procedures that allow charities to explain and justify their reserves policies and levels – these to be taken into account when grant awards are determined.

• The trustees must decide on the kinds of grants they are normally prepared to make and whether they will invite applications or find other methods of identifying potential beneficiaries.

• When applications are numerous, the trustees will need to reduce these to manageable proportions, perhaps by dividing the task of detailed consideration between various members of the trustee body.

• It is often wise to check on an applicant's other sources of funds or income, including the effects that assistance from the trust may have on statutory or other benefits. In some cases, grants by instalments and/or on conditions may be sensible for both donor and donee.

• Monitoring of the actual use of funds should be through regular questionnaires and, where feasible, unannounced spot-checks. At the same time the trustees should endeavour to limit expenses to what is essential to keep the administrative wheels in motion. This, of course, is largely a matter of judgement for each trustee body.

Trustees of grant-making trusts are not governmental bodies disbursing taxpayers' money under statutory or other controls. Within the terms of their trust, and bearing in mind the warnings given in their very different ways by Bishop Butler in the eighteenth century and the trustees of the Diana, Princess of Wales Memorial Fund in the twentieth, trustees have the capacity to be pragmatic, open-minded, imaginative, even unorthodox and, above all, independent. In the end, intuition and experience often come to be the most critical components in any of their managerial or grant-making decisions.

References

Effectiveness and the Voluntary Sector, National Council for Voluntary Organisations, 1990

Effectiveness and the Voluntary Sector On Trust Regulators Study, Charity Reserves (R53), The Charity Commission, 2003

CHAPTER THREE

Trusts as funding partners

Christopher Carnie

Introduction

Trusts and foundations are in a period of rapid change – it's the most exciting, stimulating time in recent history to be engaged in the sector – so this chapter is best seen as a snapshot of how things are in spring 2010.

The current theme is partnership. That's not how it was in the first edition of this book. Then, it was all about fundraising. But in the last 10 years we have seen a seismic change in the formerly placid world of trusts and foundations, and it's now clear that a partnership approach is the way forward.

Trust, foundation, grantmaker . . .

The word 'trust' causes confusion among people both inside and outside the fundraising world. And the addition of 'grantmaking' adds to the confusion.

For Susie, Head of Fundraising at the Fight Cancer Fund, the Esmée Fairbairn Charitable Trust is clearly a grant-making trust, and Cancer Research UK (CR-UK) is clearly a fundraising competitor.

For David, Professor of Oncology at Rutland University, CR-UK is a grantmaker that supports his research lab with generous donations each year. So is the Esmée Fairbairn Foundation.

In UK legislation both bodies (Esmée Fairbairn and CR-UK) are 'charitable trusts'. The law does not distinguish, at least at the point of registration, between grant-making and fundraising organisations. It is fundraisers who have allocated the (increasingly) arbitrary title of 'grantmaker' to around 8,800 UK charitable trusts.

In the rest of Europe this distinction is simpler. Both Esmée Fairbairn and CR-UK would simply be 'foundations.' Foundations in Europe cover a wide range of third sector activities, including running hospitals, giving grant-aid to museums or managing family wealth. In certain countries foundations do not have to be primarily or even partly charitable to qualify for the title – so it is good to know that there is a movement, led by the European Foundation Centre, to develop a common European definition of 'foundations' that would be charitable in intent.

In the US, 'private foundation' refers to a non-profit body that meets the requirements of the Internal Revenue Service (www.irs.gov) under Section 501(c)(3) of the Internal Revenue Code. In simplified form, for such a 'private foundation' to retain its status it must spend at least 85% of its net income on charitable activities. This is part of the reason why the US foundation sector is so important in fundraising in America and, increasingly, also over here too.

Various organisations, including CAF and a number of community foundations, allow donors to create subsidiary trusts. These may appear to have the name of a donor (e.g. The Chris Carnie Trust) but are in fact donor-directed funds under the shelter of the registered charity (in this case, CAF). This model of providing a donor-directed funds service also occurs in the rest of Europe; in France the Fondation de France manages more than 700 such trusts.

Community foundations are an increasingly important source of support. As the name implies, they support local charitable causes, typically by channelling donations from a number of sources to selected projects. According to the Community Foundation Network (www.community foundations.org.uk) at the time of writing there are 57 community foundations in the UK, distributing about £70 million per year in grants.

The neat labels we've been used to in fundraising – trust, company, individual donor – are also looking increasingly porous. There are a number of trusts that own companies (Bosch, the car parts manufacturer, for example) and new forms of trust–social enterprise partnerships that are breaking down these old compartments. At our research company Factary we now refer to 'strategic funders' as a coherent market segment including trusts and foundations, companies and philanthropic individuals.

Don't forget the various other places that the word 'trust' can appear. 'Private trust' could refer to money or property held in a legal trust for the benefit of children or grandchildren. This is likely to be managed by the family lawyer and will have no charitable intent.

To make this brief chapter readable, I am going to focus on organisations whose principal activity is to be a funding partner for organisations, by giving grants, loans or other support. I will simply call these entities 'trusts'.

Size of the sector

In 2009/10 there were around 9,000 trusts and foundations in the UK, with the largest 500 giving around £2.6 billion a year (DSC, 2010), an amount that puts trusts ahead of government spending in the sector (around £2.15 billion a year, according to figures from the *Government Funding Guide,*

DSC, 2010) and, importantly, more than five times the estimated £500 million of cash donations by companies a year (DSC, 2010).

The sector is powerful, financially. In 2009/10 the total assets of the top 500 trusts and foundations reached £33 billion (DSC, 2010). In asset terms, the UK is the third largest foundation market in Europe, behind only Germany (24% larger by assets, in comparable 2005 figures from *Facts and Figures*, EFC, Brussels, 2008) and Italy (76% larger by assets). Continental Europe broadly reflects the top-heavy foundation market that we have in the UK – overall the top 50 foundations in Europe hold 37% of all the assets (*Family Foundation Giving Trends 2010*, Alliance Publishing Trust, 2010).

There are some clear areas of preference, with social care (18% of grants by value, representing an estimated total £489 million, according to *Grantmaking by UK Trusts and Foundations* (CAF and ACF, 2007), health (17%), education (10%) and arts and culture (8%) being the most favoured. These figures reflect the broader European experience, where health, social services, international development and arts and culture are the top four by expenditure (*Facts and Figures*, EFC, Brussels, 2008).

Trustees' selection policies

This is the sort of heading you expect to see in a book on trusts; a quick guide to the ways in which trustees select grant recipients. Like everything else in the trusts world it's not that simple.

Why? For three reasons. First, trustees are often hardly involved in the selection process. Second because 'policy' is too definite a word to attach to the magical and obscure process by which some trusts select charity recipients. Third because trusts may want to work alongside you rather than in the traditional grantmaker/grantee relationship.

Some trusts, typically but not necessarily the largest, have a staff who make the selections. These are 'application-driven' trusts – meaning that they have an established procedure for grantseekers. Fill in the form, meet the criteria, and boom, you're in the money. These selection and due diligence processes are becoming increasingly sophisticated. In part this is the result of growing professionalism in the sector; there is now a body of people who are actively managing their portfolio of grants. There are also new tools becoming available to grantmakers – ranging from clear measures of poverty based on household classification data, through to SROI (social return on investment). SROI is a tool originally devised by venture philanthropists – donors who are applying venture capital methods to the philanthropic world. SROI seeks to quantify, and then place a value upon, the social change that occurs as the result of your work. The 'return' is the value of that social change compared with the original 'investment' or grant. For more on this see the position paper *SROI for funders* by New Philanthropy Capital at www.philanthropycapital.org/publications.

These systems help to ensure that there can be no hint of patronage about trust giving and were designed to promote equality of opportunity among grantseekers. Unfortunately they sometimes have the reverse effect, where the largest, most powerful charities employ consultants who know the selection criteria (in some cases the very consultants who *wrote* the criteria) to boost their chances.

Many trusts are not 'application-driven'. In these cases a group of trustees meets to discuss applications received and select this month/year/ quarter's batch of recipients. These boards of trustees can consist simply of a wealthy trust-founder and her lawyer; a group of friends; or an accountant or lawyer acting on the wishes of the (late) trust founder. (As a fundraiser, this last group can be the trickiest to work with – they tend to be too busy really to consider applicants and too cautious to do anything other than interpret the founder's trust deed to the letter – their giving practices are often deeply conservative.)

These groups all have one feature in common. They are human beings affected, like the rest of us, by today's earthquake or tomorrow's poor, sick child. Their giving reflects these trends, and it is artificial, in these 'non-application' trusts, to distinguish between giving by trusts and giving by individual philanthropists. Think about how you would approach a potential major donor individually – one person talking to another – and use this to help guide your approach to the trust.

Sadly, many fundraisers continue to believe that trusts are a target at which one can throw mass-produced letters. Trustees complain, with justification, that a simple listing in a directory will mean that they get hundreds of applications each week, the majority hopelessly inappropriate. While a few trusts try to hide their existence from the public, most take the sensible view that a clear description of the trust's interests and objects and a clear statement of whether they will accept unsolicited applications, ought to be enough to ensure that they get on-target applications.

Trusts as a fundraising source

What are the pros and cons of using trusts as a key fundraising source?

Strengths

● Grant-making trusts exist to, yes, make grants. This should make them top of the list for any fundraising programme.

● The increasing availability of information on the sector, including directories, databases and statistical information, makes it easier to research and to benchmark.

• According to the Centre for Interfirm Comparisons' 2008 study of fundraising, trust fundraising is the most cost-effective form of fundraising available, with a return of £9.42 in voluntary income for each £1 invested. Despite this return on investment it is the Cinderella of the fundraising budget, with just 1.8% of fundraising budgets being allocated to trusts fundraising.

• Trust fundraising can, at least in smaller organisations, be combined with other tasks. In 55% of charities, according to the 2009 Blackbaud State of the Non-profit Industry UK survey, grant-writing is a part-time occupation.

• Trust fundraising is a systematic, steady process, creating a relatively stable, long-term source of funds for your organisation. With grant sizes averaging £4,000 (Centre for Interfirm Comparisons, 2008) it's also efficient.

Weaknesses

• Trustees are professional grantmakers who will not, generally, be wooed by over-emotional appeals, figures and projections that look unrealistic or a sloppy approach. It takes care and effort to write a trust application.

• Organisations still 'silo' their trust fundraising, separating it from corporate or major donor fundraising. To understand why you shouldn't do this, see 'Putting together a trusts team' on page 25.

• Many, if not most, trust grants are restricted to a project or activity. Unrestricted funding occurs, but is rare.

Opportunities

• It's a growing sector. Factary's *New Trust Update*, which tracks the creation of new trusts in the UK, reported on 240 newly created grant-making trusts in 2009. This growth by volume is reflected in growth by value; the Centre for Interfirm Comparisons' 2008 study of fundraising showed a 15.3% growth by value from trusts fundraising from 2007 to 2008, the highest growth rate of any form of fundraising in that year. (The previous three-year average growth had been 8%.)

• Partnerships with trusts can bring you more than just money. They can add to your voice for change, working with government and business to bring about the social or environmental change you seek. (For more on this, see *More than Money: The Potential of Cross Sector Relationships*, Diana Leat, The Big Lottery Fund, 2009.)

• Think about the board of trustees' networks of contacts: you may start to open up opportunities to find new contacts.

• Winning trusts as partners can in turn bring further trust funding. Showing potential funders that you are well supported by mainstream trusts will help your applications.

• A cadre of professional trust managers is developing and with it systems for managing the selection of grant recipients. It is becoming more possible, with larger trusts, to predict where the money will go. That means better targeting, reducing waste and cost.

• Trusts outside the UK are an increasingly important market. UK fundraisers are only now beginning to understand the potential of the huge markets in Switzerland, Germany, France and, of course, the US. India, the Middle East and Asia are also increasingly interesting markets.

Threats

• Lack of public access to trust information in Scotland and Northern Ireland (as well as in certain other European countries including the Netherlands) means that key markets are not being considered. More importantly, the lack of transparency is undermining confidence in trusts and allowing some to operate in ways that are unethical and, in some cases, illegal.

• Administrative overload; too many trusts are drowning in inappropriate applications.

• Many trusts rely on a base of assets that, when the Stock Exchange is under-performing or property prices are falling, can reduce their grant-making capacity.

Putting together a trusts team

Don't. Not a 'trusts team.' At least not one that works on its own, in a tidy but isolated back room at your head office.

Instead, put together a strategic fundraising team – a group of people who work together across the key strategic funding markets – philanthropists, trusts and companies. Why? Because these three markets are intimately interconnected. It really is important that your team can share the fact that George and Jane Hedgefond are the settlors of the Hedgefond Charitable Trust, the same G&J Hedgefond who are the 85% owners of Hedgefond Ltd, the profitable financial sector business, and that George Hedgefond is the donor of a modest £1,000 per annum whom your major gifts fundraiser wants to invite to dinner in the hope that he will make a major upgrade. It's vital, if you want to win George and Jane and all the other wealthy philanthropists out there, that your organisation is capable of this type of joined-up thinking.

Fundraising from tomorrow's trusts

We are living through a period of rapid, probably accelerating, change in the trusts sector. Predictions are perilous.

Key forces at play in the sector include the shift toward more structured philanthropy, the law, the growing body of professional managers in the sector and the venture philanthropy movement.

Philanthropically minded people are increasingly structuring and consolidating their giving, and trusts provide a vehicle for doing that. This is one of the reasons behind the continued growth in the trusts sector and the increasing sophistication of trust management. Fundraisers need to match that growing sophistication with appeals that make the business case for their cause.

Changes in the law are encouraging the growth of the foundation sector in Europe. In France, for example, laws passed in 2003 created a very favourable tax situation for people making donations to new or existing foundations and consequently foundation numbers are growing. A significant change will come if the European Foundation Centre manages to persuade the European Parliament to accept its proposals for a European statute on foundations. A shift at European level will be reflected in changes in national legislation.

In the first edition of this book I wrote that those who '... create grant-making trusts . . . can look forward to a cleaner, clearer contractual relationship with their fundraising clients'. This, largely, has turned out to be the case. We are, for better or worse, in a period in which trusts and fundraising organisations interact formally, agreeing to deliver set social or environmental benefits in exchange for a grant paid over in tranches. This formality is linked to an increasing professionalism of trust management.

Venture philanthropy

The most exciting revolution in trusts in Europe is the growth of the venture philanthropy movement. Started as a new model by the then Peninsula Community Foundation (now part of the Silicon Valley Community Foundation), it applies the methods of venture capital to the world of philanthropy. This means finding non-profit organisations that are doing something interesting but whose growth is limited by a lack of capacity, and injecting money, help, advice, board members and in-kind resources to build the organisation's capacity, with the target of growing the non-profit rapidly. It's a way of multiplying the benefit to society, and it has spawned a whole new language as well as tools (including SROI), that will be of permanent benefit to the sector. Venture philanthropy is growing from a zero base – it's still a tiny percentage of the market – but it is influencing some of the biggest foundations in Europe.

Think about working with trusts, in the round. You want to create social or environmental change. So do they. How could you best work together to create the most change, the greatest social return on your collective investment? What does the trust have (contacts, influence, experience, networks – and money) that could help you achieve the change you both seek? That's the future of trusts as funding partners – working together for change.

References

Facts and Figures, EFC, Brussels, 2008

Family Foundation Giving Trends 2010, Alliance Publishing Trusts, 2010

Government Funding Guide, DSC, Sarah Johnston, 2010

Grantmaking by UK Trusts and Foundations, CAF and ACF, 2007

More than Money: The Potential of Cross Sector Relationships, Diana Leat, The Big Lottery Fund, 2009

New Trust Update, Factary Centre for Interfirm Comparisons' 2008 study of fundraising, 2009 Blackbaud State of the Non-profit Industry UK survey

PART TWO

The Critical Importance of Research and Planning

CHAPTER FOUR

Identifying and locating trusts

Kay Holmes-Siedle

Introduction

Locating, identifying and researching trusts is where any good trust fundraiser begins his or her work, after having gained in-depth knowledge of the charity's work and being clear about the different types of trust that are to be found in the UK and overseas. This chapter is intended to help trust fundraisers understand the nature, scope, detail and planning needed to undertake and successfully complete the research phase.

Before we begin the business of identifying and locating relevant trusts, let us take the time to consider a number of facts that we must bear in mind during our research exercise:

• Many charitable trusts in this country are vehicles for an individual, a family and/or the relatives of the deceased settlor to enjoy philanthropy. To misunderstand this key fact and disregard researching the trustees will lead to severe under-performance.

• An organisation called a 'trust', 'foundation' or 'charity' is not necessarily a grant-making body. It could be a family tax-avoidance vehicle, a government foundation (particularly relevant overseas), or a charity that raises money for financing projects it has established itself.

• Additionally, not all trusts that make grants to charities are registered with the relevant regional charity commission as charitable trusts. Many are individuals using a tax vehicle called a trust who do not want the intrusion of public scrutiny. This will necessarily restrict what can be discovered about them and their activities, but from the name and address we may be able to discover information about the key decision-maker.

Phase 1 – Internal sources, auditing your existing supporters

Most charities should be undertaking an annual internal audit of the trusts, foundations, settlements and other grant-making bodies that support them. Some that are better resourced may, of course, be able to monitor their trust-giving on a more active basis, say monthly or quarterly, after the initial audit.

The purpose of the audit is to enable you, the trust fundraiser, to discover the answers to these key questions:

• Do you know about all of the trusts that have supported your charity, in the last five years?

• Which are the most generous trusts by single gift and by cumulative gift? Are they giving at the top of their capacity to you?

• Do you hold sufficient information to place each trust in gift bands within a gift pyramid? You can only do this accurately if you consider their fit to your case/charity's objectives, grant size, biographies of the key trustees and your charity networks to the key decision-making trustees.

• How many trusts that currently support your charity are not listed and described in the main reference sources? Do you recognise the opportunity to capitalise on these findings?

• How quickly does your charity classify a supporter as lapsed? Could this have led to some trusts being prematurely deleted from your charity's trust lists? This can be particularly pertinent following the completion of a capital campaign, with outside volunteers managing the records. Are any of them listed in past annual reports?

• Have you sufficient trusts to meet your targets or do you need to undertake prospect research?

• Do you know your success rate in approaching and securing a gift (and, for the sophisticated fundraisers, at the level at which you asked)? It is important that you know this, as it will clearly influence how many trusts you need to locate in each gift band (for example, it might be 1:2 for existing trusts and 1:4 for new prospect trusts).

• Can you already identify (by eye) that there are trusts missing from the existing supporter lists?

How to research your existing supporters to maximise your gift opportunities

1. Re-read your case for support/programme/project proposals before you start. It is vital that you have the knowledge to be able to check that your objectives meet the objectives of the trust, or at the very least are not now excluded because of a change in your work or their objectives.

2. Take your income target for one year or the number of years you wish to cover, draw up a current gift chart or pyramid (showing the number of gifts/grants required in value ranges, for example. 1@£100,000, 2@£50,000, 4@£20,000), placing your current supporters by name and mean gift size into the chart. If you have hundreds of trust donors put the numbers in the lower value gift bands.

3. Assemble all the information that you can about the trust supporters have given to you in the last three years. You can repeat this exercise or extend it to cover five years. Look for all trusts, not just those in your current portfolio, by searching your direct marketing database by key word, for example trust, foundation; check capital appeal lists that may have been created by regional committees and your corporate fundraising department for company trusts, as they may now be focusing on, for example, charity of the year and trade-linked promotions.

4. What you do next will depend to an extent on your resources and budgets. So you may need to adapt the scale of the exercise described next.

5. Take your top 50–100 most generous trust supporters by single gift and undertake research using your internal files, the Charity Commission (or Charity Regulator in Scotland) and the trusts' websites to gather detail on their grants budgets and grants lists for the last five years, the names of, and any information about, their trustees, their objectives and longevity (for example, has the trust only a limited time left to run?). Opportunities can arise if you can see that a trust has a large asset base left to dispose of for charitable purposes and only two years to accomplish the task.

6. Undertake biographical profiling of the key trustees, where you do not already have this in your internal files. Key trustees (the key decision-makers) would be the settlor or trustee, the husband and wife of a personal trust, the next generation relations of an in-memoriam trust.

7. Where there are no obvious key trustees you will need to profile all the trustees, looking for information that suggests a close fit with your charity. A trust with wide objectives may have a broad range of people to help it make decisions in particular areas of interest. (As a past administrator of a trust I knew exactly which trustee on my board I wanted to read any given proposal and I could often guess with some

accuracy which proposals would receive support, given their personal interests.) If you have not already done so, establish who is, or who could be, the route or network to each key trustee, using your internal networks such as your trustees, key staff and development board or fundraising committee.

8. Gift grade each trust, using all of the information at your disposal, for example what each trust could give you based on its full capacity, not just past gifts to you, its warmth and connections to you and its fit to your current case. If you have not undertaken gift grading consider getting some consultancy help the first time around. Similarly, if you cannot undertake the trustee research, buy in some external help – it is vital you know about the trustees: this knowledge will pay dividends.

9. Now take the rest of your trust list. If there is insufficient time and resources to do the rest of the audit in one go, set yourself an appropriate gift target; for example, aim to identify all trusts that could give a gift of £20,000 or over and look at the grants budget and grants lists for this data first, set aside those trusts that cannot meet this objective and complete the research exercise as described above.

You are now in a position to complete next year's gift chart and see the scale of the income gap, remembering to factor in your success rate, for example, it will probably be necessary to identify two warm donors (or whatever your charity's success rate is) for every gift sought at the level of £20,000.

Note: You may be questioning why you should bother with all this research when you could just compare your lists with research that is available on one of the various online research sources. If you do this you will of course get exactly the same snapshot and the same trusts as your competitors. You will also fail to gain the in-depth information necessary to cultivate your top donors for top gifts. Have you ever wondered why some charities seem to be at the top of the grants lists? In our experience it is rarely through luck and mainly through thorough research and excellent approaches.

Caveat: By setting aside smaller trusts you may miss opportunities with new personal trusts or trusts which are the public face of a wealthy individual's philanthropy. You could consider commissioning an external agency with good trustee information to identify any gems.

Phase 2 – Prospecting for new trusts

Once you have completed your internal audit you will have learnt a great deal that will be helpful in drawing up your prospect research brief:

● You should know how many new trusts you need to locate and for what gift levels. Again you need to bear in mind your success rate with cold trusts.

● You should know your case for support, your programmes and projects and the different ways in which you might be able to 'sell' them to a donor. For example, you might be able emphasise your Christian credentials; the economic as well as, or instead of, the social value of the work you do with homeless people; the way in which your projects offer training and empowerment rather than just welfare. All these emphases allow you to become more sophisticated in drawing up the selection criteria for identifying new trusts and, sometimes more importantly, the trustees' interests.

● You should know what networks you have to what types of people, for example whether you are strong on City of London connections but weak on rural county connections. Or you might have a well-known 40-year-old entrepreneur on your development board or fundraising committee who is very comfortable approaching anyone in the IT, equity or media business.

● You may even have converted some of your most generous donors into advocates on your behalf and increased your networks still further.

Here is an example of some of the key words/emphases that we took into account when we drew up an internal research brief for a heritage project after reading all of the case for support information and visiting the project.

● Heritage
● Restoration/preservation
● Museums
● History (Victorian)
● Maritime interests
● Shipping
● Engineering
● Design
● Industrial archaeology

● Education
● Disabled access
● Royal family
● 'Best of British'
● National interest
● Navy
● Geographic location
● Self interest
● Gifts in kind

Additionally, we determined that in this case prospects needed to be capable of gifts of £20,000 or over.

You are now ready to start your prospect research with whatever sources you have at your disposal. Again, try not to use all the same sources as your competitors and do undertake trustee research.

The strategies I have outlined above are tried and tested recipes for success – I know from over 30 years' experience that individuals are the key to success, especially for personal approaches but also for written proposals. The appropriate information presented in the right tone of voice and style can make a huge difference.

CHAPTER FIVE

Preparing projects for trust approaches

Redmond Mullin

Introduction

Trust or foundation approaches, like the rest of fundraising, demand persuasive communications. Therefore their design, together with the selection of projects and the propositions to be made, must start with understanding these sources and the ways in which relations with them can be made optimally productive. The principles stated here apply to not-for-profit organisations of all types and sizes.

Personal contacts

Decisions are made by people, whether individually or in committee. The majority of trusts are channels through which rich individuals and families make their contributions to not-for-profit causes. But even where the person or people to be dealt with is a trust administrator, or one or more trustees, there is a strong personal element in their decision-making. Here are three examples:

• A medium-sized family trust meets twice yearly in its chair's home in the Cotswolds. Regular grants are reported on and reappraised. The recipients have been visited by the part-time director. New candidates are proposed for support: all but the smallest have been visited. There is a report by the director on the small grants made at his discretion. If an application is beyond the available means of this trust, other family members who have trusts of their own may decide to collaborate by making grants up to the level needed.

• One of the great English philanthropic families, with several major trusts, meets to consider a major funding application. Father, mother, son and cousin are there, with the trusts' formal administrators. The applicant charity's representatives are there. The discussion is open. The father strongly argues for addition of a new element to the programmes proposed. When he questions another aspect of the appeal, his son promptly agrees to fund this from his own trust, to avoid argument. The full, composite grant is made.

• The president of a foundation which bears his name, of which he is not even named as a trustee, personally makes the main decisions about grants. Apart from his own projects, this has brought £300,000 in response to a press photograph of a heritage emergency, and payments of development fees, where these could be constructive for his chosen organisations.

The situation with more institutionally managed trusts or foundations is different but the personal element remains important. This is evident to anyone who has close, perhaps regular, contact with helpful trustees or trust directors. My focus switches to their viewpoint. As director of two grant-making advisory committees, I was generally more vividly and better informed in discussing an application when there had been a meeting with key representatives of the organisation concerned. As a member of the Gulbenkian Foundation's Arts Initiative and Money (AIM) programme, I found that the quality of our grant allocations depended on an interview or site visit (my *AIM Report*, published by the Calouste Gulbenkian Foundation in 1984, demonstrates this.) The point is obvious: best decisions are taken where the case is strong, the argument is vividly and directly made and the supporting information has been discussed.

Typologies of trusts

I hope some preliminary matters have been established. Already hinted at is a crude typology of trusts, which needs to be considered before communication starts. One conclusion of a flawed investigation undertaken some years ago was that there were significant differences in behaviour between the largest trusts, which had secretariats; medium-sized trusts, which might or might not be professionally managed; and small trusts, which might be managed by a solicitor or accountant (*Report on Foundation Activity*, Booth & Mullin, CAF, 1976). Those distinctions remain partly valid but do not allow for the impact of actively concerned trustees on any trust's decision-making. Nor do they allow for special factors, such as a founding family's interest in a particular place or region. During the campaign to establish the new university in Lincoln, a virtually unknown, small family trust came forward at a press launch and expressed interest. The family had decided to wind up the trust. The appeal received £250,000 as a result.

This suggests some more functionally useful distinctions: between trusts which are either personal or institutional in character, and between those whose decisions are usually or on occasion personally determined or bureaucratically determined. A further, critical distinction, given the emphasis I have placed on personal relations, is between trusts where contact can be established and those where it is unattainable.

Support for the trust application

The case for support must be clearly described first

↓

The case for support opens the channel for people to give to people; the basis of all charitable giving and support

↓

Two key skills of importance in writing the case for support are clarity and brevity. Cover the following points:

↓

Who you are, when you were established, and where you are

↓

What you were set up to do ('homelessness' is not an adequate description)

Address your reason for being by describing your work

↓

Speak in terms of individuals, not labelled beneficiary groups

↓

Do not assume that the trustees will understand your jargon, know anything about you or speak in the politically correct language which is second nature in the voluntary sector

↓

What is the ratio of salaried to unpaid workers?

↓

Quantify your work (counselling service – how many clients/number of hours spent with them?)

Factors affecting decisions

This preliminary scan of some desirable relations with trusts is needed for the direction of my main argument to be understood. If, almost regardless of the type of trust concerned, there are strong personal factors influencing grant decisions, then the grant proposition must allow for them. Trustees and trust directors, however perfect the criteria and procedures established to guide them, are affected by personal contact and knowledge, and by general prejudices for and against certain causes. Some trust decision-makers are prepared to provide funding for difficult objects, such as overheads, salaries and fees; many, initially at least, are not. Most decision-makers and influencers will be inclined in favour of great ideas and the programmes which embody them, whether these are on a massive or limited scale.

Aims and targets for trust propositions

This is where the more mechanical section of this chapter begins. As a not-for-profit organisation starts on an appeal or on preparing a set of funding propositions, directed perhaps only to trusts or foundations but more often also to individual and corporate sources, it must be clear on the outcomes to be achieved through the sums it seeks, the overall sum to achieve them and the units of support it needs within that overall sum, source by source. Most frequently, the intended outcomes will be specific: the funding of a building, equipment, a project or a component within a broad programme. Occasionally, the cause itself and the related appeal, strongly declared, may attract significant units of support that are designated to no specific purpose. However, even if your organisation is one which, with little effort, sometimes attracts large, undesignated support, you must still have articulated a cause of significance, with projects and programmes that will have a positive impact on it. In all instances, the funding proposition must carry the assent of the organisation's key staff and trustees.

Selection of trust sources

The organisation must also decide on the sources of funding it should approach. These may include individuals, often through their trusts and companies. A very simple principle for selection applies here: if a trust or foundation's stated objects preclude any form of support for the organisation's cause or remit (for example in terms of the people or region which may benefit) then it should not waste the trust's/foundation's and its time making a grant application. Normally, the same restriction will apply even if the trust's mutable (changeable) policies preclude an approach – unless the strength of the case or personal contact might change or by-pass those policies.

The funding proposition

It is when the proposition is brought together with the prospective source that the fund-raiser's judgement and skill are proved. I assume that the proposition will be supported by a business plan and budget projections. But while the proposition derives from a broad plan of action, it will be articulated for a particular source or group of sources. It will be specific for them. The trustee or administrator who receives what is obviously a randomly distributed appeal, perhaps opening with 'Dear Sir or Madam' and supported by a glossy brochure, will almost certainly discard it. On the other hand, the prospectus or proposal document should not assume knowledge of the cause or service or use any jargon.

A trust's decision-making is likely to involve a delicate process and applicants for funds are at an advantage if their contact with the grant-giving organisation starts positively. Even with those trusts that sometimes give impulsively, the message must be clear and motivating if it is to trigger the response desired. And allowance must be made for prejudice as well as ignorance. Certain causes or fields of activity may be instinctively disliked or misunderstood: for example, even in recent years projects for misusers, addicts and even homeless single parents have been relatively difficult to fund. The significance of other causes may have been inadequately appreciated: for example, mental disability, epilepsy and AIDS programmes. Then there are the perennially difficult issues relating to overheads, administrative and promotional costs.

None of those negative factors need be overwhelming. Intelligent drafting can make an obscure case clear. With insight, the propositions can be framed so that they address ignorance or low awareness. Indeed, the relative unpopularity of a cause or activity can become a positive point in the argument for its support. It may be shown that a valuable project can succeed only if it receives support from this and a few other singularly sympathetic trusts.

Overheads: an issue

Issues concerning overheads are always with us. Many trusts are more realistic about them now than they used to be, and some, such as the main medical research charities and many trusts with primarily academic objects, have agreed common policies on them. Where the argument must be re-entered, some points can be clearly stated. Many organisations have made difficulties for themselves by saying: 'Here are the essential costs of services' and 'There are the administrative and promotional costs' – thus creating a situation where the source may choose to give support to the former but not to the latter. If an organisation has overheads which do not relate directly to, and make possible, services, those overheads may legitimately be questioned – whether the services relate to social work, opera, an academic department, a hospital. The fact that a service cannot be delivered unless the essential overheads are provided is something that can be shown. Of course, with some more sympathetic and better informed trusts this is not an issue. Quite recently one trust elected specifically to fund a department's overheads because it might be difficult to attract support for them;

another trust opted to pay for an organisation's promotional costs; another volunteered to pay for a college's consultancy fees for a funding study. In one instance the trust's decision-maker gave £1 million to establish whether a revolutionary project was viable.

The application

As the more mechanical aspects of putting together grant applications to trusts are considered, the related points made in the previous paragraph must be kept in mind. The intention is to deliver a persuasive argument, not to complete a tedious routine. Some trusts and foundations have created forms to be completed for applications. Even these give scope for the kind of persuasion, based on the fundraiser's insight, which I have been discussing. My emphasis now is on the components of an application where a standard application form is not provided. I am not laying down strict rules here: a variety of forms of approach may be apt. Creativity is involved. And it can be an advantage if there is an established relationship with the trust approached – where there may be discussion about a proposition before any formal approach is made and possibly help in formulating the proposition. Yet, even where there is a close relationship, some formalities will usually need to be observed in the concluding stages of the application. And, as I have said, personal contact may not be possible. Success is feasible without it.

A crucial component in the application, and the first to be considered by the trustee or administrator to whom the application is sent, is the letter or summary proposition which introduces the application for support. With this your argument may be lost or partly won. It does not need to include all the evidence backing your case but it does need to make the case convincingly, allowing for the recipient's likely understanding and attitudes. The letter or summary also needs to be succinct. Normally I would not want to exceed two sides of A4 paper, with four as an extreme, and this only if the case were tightly argued. This is not because recipients are lazy; but they are exposed to many applications and need to make their preliminary decisions promptly.

Moreover, if the trust has even simple bureaucratic procedures, the administrator will have to include the summary, but not usually the full documentation, in papers for the trustees' meeting at which a decision may be made. Frequently, the first intention of the application would be to secure an interview or visit from principal decision-makers or their representatives. The letter summarising the proposition or which accompanies the summary should be signed by someone of standing with the organisation (chair, director, faculty head, senior curator) not by a fundraiser or a member of another department unless that is where the relationship with a trust is well established.

The application needs to be specific on the funding requirement. It is silly to expect a trust to guess the scale and timing of funding needed, and it is a nuisance for the administrator to get back in touch to find out. This means that the sum sought must be stated and justified, and the incidence of the need be known, for example in a project spread over three or four years, where progressive payments can be made, or where a grant two years hence (perhaps for a trust currently totally committed) would be as effective as a grant now. It follows that the application must also indicate what funding is anticipated from other sources, to put this grant in context, unless the request is for full funding of a project, salary or capital scheme. Finally, the application must show, in relation to a capital grant, that the enterprise will be viable once established or, with a revenue project, that after the period of a grant (three or four years, for example) it will have the means to continue.

Evidently, there is more information proposed than can be included in a letter or summary, although this must cover the main points. Therefore there must usually be a set of supporting papers and documents, to substantiate claims and provide the detailed information required:

● There will in many cases need to be a full, technical description of the project or programme. The trust decision-maker may often use expert assessors where the application is of some complexity. For a capital programme, architectural plans or equipment specifications will be needed. There may also need to be illustrations or visualisations of buildings or objects, even DVDs to help those decision-makers understand what is intended. These support documents may be in the form of a detailed research proposal or a business prospectus, which is my preference above a fine brochure, unless the project relates to a gallery, opera house or other such enterprise, where that style might be appropriate.

● There will usually need to be a statement of vision and mission, a related business plan and projections over three to four years of anticipated income, with its sources, and of expenditure, with its incidence and purposes. This part of the application will include a description of the organisation's aims and achievements.

● Accounts and, if possible, the annual report should be provided. You may need to state and explain the ratios of fundraising costs to income. Unless included elsewhere, there should be lists of trustees and senior staff, with an outline of the organisation's governance. Of course, a request for emergency funds cannot observe all these formalities; in such a case the passion and weight of argument must succeed.

Selection of trusts

Everything discussed in this chapter concerns the interaction between an applicant and a possible provider of funds. For the fundraiser, this means that there must be apt selection followed by the best possible understanding of prospective trust sources and their principal decision-makers. There is basic research, using the standard directories and professional agencies, which can help with this. But the information they can provide is limited, particularly where the personal interests and prejudices of these decision-makers are concerned. Organisations which already have good relations with at least a few trusts start with an advantage. Those which do not may be able to get advice on the attitudes and behaviour of trusts and foundations they believe might respond to them. Otherwise quite raw decisions must be made: on who might respond to a capital appeal for buildings or equipment; for research or medical or welfare projects; for a university department or arts body. Some may be able to consider foundations outside the UK.

External factors

There are external events which affect all funding decision-makers, and their concerns must be considered. Government policies periodically change the availability of statutory funding for crucial categories of people in need: homeless people, lone parents, people needing expensive treatments for cancer and other conditions, young people needing funds for secondary or tertiary education excluded from public support, for whatever reason. Many trustees have felt that they should not respond to pressures created by government's decision to remove support they perceive the government should provide. And then they are confronted with people in desperate situations who will not receive the support they need unless these trustees, perhaps exceptionally concerned and enlightened, decide to provide it. Lottery funds are making often impossible demands on organisations without fundraising achievement or skills to raise sometimes millions of pounds in partnership funds. I often say that good fundraising changes the realities. Some individual organisations may be able to change the policies of a few trusts. Otherwise there needs to be wider-scale persuasion, involving many organisations in a common cause.

Consolidation

Another point I have made is that it is productive for an organisation to establish firm relations with trusts which have supported it and may continue to do so. Such relations can be cultivated. Of course, the organisation must keep its trusts as well as its other supporters informed about what their funds have achieved. Trustees and administrators can constructively be kept in touch with progress, through meetings, site visits and other contacts. They can also remain involved through occasional consultation and by taking them into the organisation's confidence on issues and developments. Most trust supporters like to be valued in such ways.

Should we have a trust department? – an issue

Finally, there are structural matters to be considered by any organisation which undertakes trust fundraising. I have argued that most trusts are the vehicles used by individuals or families for their philanthropic transactions, so that there needs to be good understanding of a trust's decision-making before approaches are made. Similar comment can be made about some corporate trusts. One question which follows from this is: should the organisation have a trust fundraising department? There can be some serious consequent problems if it does, unless it defines roles and relationships very clearly. The judgement concerns the places where optimally productive relations can be established: within a major private or corporate support function or a specific trust function. Does the trust fundraising department operate as an information-providing, coordinating function with direct responsibility for institutional trusts, which would not otherwise be covered, and perhaps for Lottery applications? Beyond this, in some organisations there may be many possible originating points for trust approaches. It is generally counterproductive to create a situation in which major trusts may receive a batch of simultaneous approaches from within the same organisation. This does not mean that all approaches should be from head office. In many instances an approach from some other point may be more effective. But the approaches do need to be coordinated.

References

AIM Report, Redmond Mullin, Calouste Gulbenkian Foundation in 1984
Report on Foundation Activity, J. D. Livingston-Booth and Redmond Mullin, CAF, 1976

CHAPTER SIX

Planning approaches

Graham Collings

Introduction

Of course you should plan trust approaches carefully. However many trusts you're going to approach, think of it as a trusts *programme* – not just a series of applications. In other words, the trusts' part of your fundraising is coordinated, balanced and focused, and with its own targets.

Don't get too carried away with the planning process. You can spend too long on planning rather than doing. I've worked with several charities where a trusts database has been researched, analysed and segmented to death, but where all the effort brought no improvement in results. Approaching trusts is basically a simple operation, and over-zealous planning or analysing should not detract from the fundamental task of making targeted approaches every month of the year.

So this might be a shorter chapter than you were expecting.

Getting the basics right

There are some basic questions to ask in planning your trusts fundraising programme.

1. What scale of trust fundraising do you need? Thinking about the overall fundraising target of your charity; how much of that could realistically be achieved from trusts? This will vary greatly from one charity to another and there is no set ratio, but just saying 'get as much as you can' is not good enough. As you will have read in previous chapters, some aspects of your charity's work will be more appealing to trusts than others. Any charity should try to maintain a balance of funding from different sources. So, however difficult it is, you ought to have a separate target for trusts.

2. How does trust fundraising fit in with the rest of your fundraising? Trusts could be 10% or 90% of the fundraising mix in your organisation, but the work needs to be coordinated with other methods. Make sure that your trusts target and deadlines dovetail with everyone else's. There should be lots of cross-pollination – shared contacts, research, feedback and project updates. Your charity's members or individual supporters could provide valuable links to trusts, for example.

3. **Who's involved?** Although the fundraiser needs to be in charge, there's a team effort required here. Your charity's trustees or committee members could be helping with contacts or feedback on project ideas. Frontline staff and volunteers must be consulted about project details and updates. Your director may want to approve and sign applications. Part of the planning is for the fundraiser to make everyone aware of their roles, and to orchestrate the whole process.

4. **What techniques will you use?** Writing letters and completing application forms is essential, but think about what you can do on the telephone or by email in terms of researching, networking, making contact and developing relationships. Is it worth holding an event to try and interest more trusts? What will you do about previous donors or the trusts which say 'no unsolicited applications'?

Making best use of your time

If trust fundraising is only one part of your job, you'll need to plan carefully to use limited time effectively. Sadly this is one of the less glamorous areas of fundraising; trusts work is often not immediate and pressing, and it's easy when you're busy to put it off. Try to remember then that your trust fundraising needs to be active 12 months of the year. Where the hare of events fundraising sprints away and then stops to take a rest, the trust fundraising tortoise plods steadily along to get even better results!

Specialist trust fundraisers also need to plan carefully in order not to miss opportunities. Trust application deadlines are coming and going every month of the year. New grant schemes or policy changes can appear at any time. You will need a schedule setting out the deadlines for relevant trusts month by month, and this will have to be matched up with your project deadlines.

Build into the schedule the time you need to spend on researching trusts, updating information, developing proposals, networking and building contacts, providing reports and feedback. All these tasks are vital to your trusts programme, as well as pushing out applications, but don't let them take over your life. If you're spending less than 50% of your trust fundraising time on doing actual applications, you probably need to rethink priorities.

Another important consideration is to balance your time between work on different types of applications, for example, approaches for core or project funding, large one-off and small regular gifts, long-term or short-term needs. An objective for any trusts programme should be to secure different types of funding from different types of trust. Putting all your eggs in one basket is a dangerous strategy. A common example is the charity with a major Lottery grant about to expire. 'Find me a big trust to replace the Lottery money' is the request that comes to the fundraiser. Well, by all means have a go, but don't neglect trusts of different types and at different levels that could make up the funding.

Putting the trusts programme together

It's easiest to think of your trusts programme in four stages, based on the traditional four stages of the fundraising cycle.

Stage one – getting proposals ready

• Clarify key facts, messages and arguments about your organisation. Why is it needed? Why is the work important? Which messages need emphasising for trusts?

• Identify what you need funds for and where trust funding – as distinct from funding from other sources – is most appropriate.

• Discuss project details with relevant staff and volunteers. Seek out information that trusts particularly look for, for example evidence of need, results and outcomes.

• Draft all materials for approaches, including, for example, graphics and photos, and make sure that copies of the most recent accounts are ready.

Stage two – researching

• Research trusts that look appropriate in terms of objects, geographical remit, deadlines and so on.

• Talk to your charity's own trustees, patrons and committee members to see if any have contacts with trusts.

• Research other supporters to identify any contacts; for example, does that major donor/long-term supporter in Birmingham know any trustees based in the West Midlands?

• Download application forms and/or guidelines where available.

• Prioritise your hit list of trusts in terms of deadlines, best prospects and availability of contacts.

Stage three – making the approaches

- Plan a manageable programme of approaches.

- Check or update trust details if needed.

- Set your contacts to work where appropriate, for example by asking them to talk to trustees or administrators.

- Write the applications, using all the information you have gathered about specific trusts to focus them correctly.

- Monitor the programme of approaches; keep an eye on deadlines.

Stage four – reviewing and following up

- Record all responses and fully update your trusts database.

- Provide updates where needed, for example where project funding has come in.

- Evaluate response rates from different types of trust, different projects and/or different types of approach.

- Say thank you.

- Spread word of your successes.

When your trusts programme is up and running, all these tasks should be progressed throughout the year and you'll have to deal with all four stages at once. But you can use this process for planning approaches for a new project, and every now and then it's worth reminding your director and/or your trustees that there is such a process. Most people think that trust fundraisers just churn out letters!

Normally trusts expect you to apply no more than once a year, so you can plan on approaching and re-approaching them with a three-year rolling programme according to their responses. There will be rejections (usually a short standard letter), and many trusts will simply not respond, but that does not necessarily mean you have wasted your time. Your approach may simply have come at a time when the trust was under financial pressure or had too many applications in a similar field to yours.

Unless the rejection is firm and clear, it's worth following a 'three strikes and out', policy of approaches before giving up on any trust prospect. Thus a three-year programme of approaches for a group of trusts might run as follows:

Year one response	Year two action	Year three action
No reply	Re-approach	Re-approach
Firm no, not eligible	No action	No action
Standard rejection	Re-approach	Re-approach
Yes	Update, re-approach	Re-approach

In all cases watch out for changes in trusts' policies in subsequent years, or for new projects run by your charity which might give you a better chance.

After three years of rejections or no response from a trust it's probably wise to call it a day. Even so, continue to monitor the trust's operations, as situations can and do change, and a new contact might make all the difference.

Planning for success

In planning your trust approaches keep in mind a few key principles:

• **Quality beats quantity** – Quality is more important than quantity in trusts fundraising. Targeting your applications closely to a trust's requirements really does make a difference, and spending the time on research and focusing is definitely worthwhile. Don't let yourself be judged solely on the volume of applications you've made; 10 well-targeted applications to good prospects should produce far more than a rushed mailshot to 100 trusts.

• **Keep up with the changes** – The trust world has become much more varied and changing in recent years. New trusts are being established all the time, while others are wound up, grant-giving policies and priorities are regularly altered and different grant programmes are introduced. This is all healthy and makes the field more interesting, but trust fundraisers need to be on their toes. Keeping track of the updates, checking websites and sharing information with other fundraisers have become essential parts of the job. No longer can you set out a hit-list of trusts in January and then just work through it until December. Every month you should be identifying new trusts to approach, researching and updating trust information and networking – which also makes the job much more interesting.

• **Batching applications** – I've always found it helpful to organise applications in batches, based around a particular project or focused on a particular type of trust, for example. Trusts in a particular batch get a similar, but not identical, type of approach, making it easier to organise the work programme and monitor the success of different approaches. This can clarify, for example, whether local trusts are responding more than non-local ones, or whether one project is more 'trust-friendly' than another.

● **Take a step back** – It's easy to get into a rut with approaches to trusts. For several years I sent a fairly standard approach to one trust and as we always got £500 in return I thought my charity was doing quite well. Then I discovered that other organisations were receiving four and five figure grants from the same trust. A phone call established that we were on the trust's list for 'small annual grants', and that it had no idea how my charity's work had developed since the £500 figure was set. A completely different approach opened the trust's eyes and it started awarding us grants of £10,000. The lesson is to take a step back every now and then and check every aspect of your trusts work. Are your proposals strong enough? Do they address topical issues? Are there different ways of making contact with trusts? What lessons are to be learned from trust responses and feedback?

● **Use your contacts** – It really is worth spending time identifying and making use of contacts. So often this part of the stage three process on page 49 is neglected, or fundraisers give up on it because the initial response is poor. Few people think they will know any trustees, and they may be reluctant to talk about their friends in this way. But I have always found that, handled correctly, this exercise yields surprisingly good results. It works well in local campaigns, where the networks are likely to be strong. It also works well if you take the trouble to research a list of potential contacts relevant to the audience, for example showing a list of trusts with a medical remit or with medically qualified trustees to a group of health professionals. The key is to keep the focus on the cause rather than the process, and remind people how easy this is. Once people are motivated and understand that a gentle, focused conversation is all that's needed rather than a browbeating rant or an hour-long presentation, then they will usually help you. Another useful technique is to bring people together as a group to look at possible trust contacts, providing refreshments and creating an enjoyable session of brainstorming and reminiscence.

A plan for proactive trusts

Trust fundraisers agonise over the ever-growing number of trusts saying 'no unsolicited applications'. How can you deal with these trusts? The numbers in this category are increasing all the time, and many very large grants are now offered by trusts that do their own research and help only specific causes with which trustees choose to be involved. Your trusts strategy can no longer afford to give up on this group.

One answer has been to send an annual report or some project information without any request for funding and hope that some of these trusts will pick up on your work. Occasionally this might succeed, perhaps mostly where the 'don't call us' message is really only a device to reduce the number of applications. However, this is just one part of the plan: the time has come for trust fundraisers to plan more thoroughly to attract the attention of proactive funders.

So how can you capture their attention? First of all it's worth remembering that they are also looking for you, and that lots of people are on the lookout for relevant causes to support. One example of the new types of trusts around is The Funding Network, which operates by bringing individual donors together to identify and support projects. This trust has a national network of 150 people actively looking for projects to fund, usually with grants of at least £5,000.

It is possible to get large grants from proactive funders. A small overseas aid charity recently had an article published in a Sunday newspaper about its plans to set up a school for orphaned children in Zambia. Three trusts responded directly to this, all previously unknown to the charity, including one which committed £100,000.

Proactive trusts are gathering information from articles in the media, internet searches, topical issues, contacts of trustees and friends and first-hand experience of a charity's work, or by researching a specific project area. So you need to have an eye open for points of contact and your charity needs to be visible in the right places. Here are some things you could do:

- Explore and use your trustee, member and supporter contacts and networks. Inform them, update them and inspire them to help you with any trust contacts they have.

- Make sure your publicity, and whoever deals with it in your organisation, includes a focus on media and messages likely to be of interest to funders. Check the feedback and responses.

- Check that your charity's entry on the Charity Commission website gives out the right messages. Funders are increasingly using this as a research tool.

- Look out for the general enquiries or information requests your charity receives. Ensure that staff and volunteers report interesting enquiries to you. This could be a trust researching you, and if so it needs to be dealt with effectively.

● Make sure that key phrases about the charity's work come up on search engines.

This may all seem unfocused compared with your normal routine of trust approaches. But it's not just about getting more publicity, it's about being alert to points of contact and making key messages and propositions for trusts more visible in the right areas. Making contact with proactive trusts need not be a major part of your work, but it's certainly worth attention as more and more grantgivers move to function in this way.

PART THREE

Approaching Grant-making Trusts

CHAPTER SEVEN
Making first contact

Tim Finn

Introduction

The project is defined, the trust research complete, the approach strategy planned with care. From this point the human factor in trust fundraising will become paramount in ensuring a successful outcome to the campaign.

It is helpful, at this stage, to remember just why the human factor in approaches to trusts plays such an important part in the results. It might be supposed that, equipped with all the documentary support compiled during the preparatory work, you are already in a position to despatch excellent written applications for your researched trusts to consider. In all logic, these should result in plentiful grants arriving. Not so. A purely written technique, a correspondence campaign, will always produce a far smaller return than a campaign that takes full account of the many personal elements at work in trusts' grant decisions.

To understand why this is the case, it will be helpful to see the subject of grant applications, not from the fundraiser's perspective, but through the eyes of one of the trusts targeted. A moment's reflection will then show just how human – how non-documentary – many of the factors at work are.

Case study of an imaginary grant-making trust

Let us take as an illustration the case of an imaginary trust of medium-to-large size, the Knatchpole Trust, whose giving objects cover a range of general, charitable themes.

The Knatchpole Trust has £1 million to distribute in grants each year. Since it seeks to donate money rather than spend its funds unnecessarily, its staff is limited to just two people: the correspondent, Mr Protheroe, and his secretary. The Knatchpole Trust receives 25 times more applications than it can possibly support. As many as 70 separate grant submissions arrive in an average week.

Mr Protheroe is a conscientious man. He endeavours to assess all the cold, written applications in the light of his trust's objectives. In truth, however, this is a near impossible task. This very morning his mailbox has yielded no fewer than 15 requests, with subject matters as diverse as Cambwick Castle Restoration, Student Homeless Outreach, the Botswana Herons' Egg Society and a children's playgroup in Polperro. All of these theoretically qualify for consideration; as to the merits of any one versus any other, it will be very difficult to make a judgement between them.

Suddenly the phone rings. It is the trust's chair, Sir Hector Knatchpole. 'Look here, I've just heard about a wonderful cause and I think we ought to support it. I've told them to write in. There should be something on your desk this morning.'

'It wouldn't be Student Homeless Outreach or Cambwick Castle Restoration, perhaps?' Mr Protheroe enquires. 'No. No. Nothing like that. It's herons' eggs in Botswana. Put it on the shortlist, will you. I think we need to look at this one pretty seriously. Far too little is being done about the Botswana heron, in my opinion.'

Sir Hector clearly has received a personal approach.

This example illustrates a broad, general principle: where applications are of apparently equal merit, trustees will often rely on the recommendations of dependable acquaintances for guidance on which charitable causes they should support.

This is why the human factor is so important. To make personal approaches to trusts, you will sometimes need to enlist specialist 'helpers' – sometimes called patrons – to open doors for you.

Final documentary preparation

Before assuming that your documentary preparations are complete, you would be wise to make sure that your researched material is not just comprehensive but that it is presented in an accessible format. Indigestible trust information can be very daunting if it has not been carefully tailored to meet its human audience.

For the purpose of discussions with helpers, prepare four separate lists of researched trusts, each strictly limited to 50 trusts at most. An interested helper will gladly consider 50 trusts and may then go on to consider 50 more – but it is important to feed the information through to the helper in manageable tranches.

The four lists of trust will normally be:

- major trusts – of national importance
- City livery companies – closely resembling major trusts
- local and regional trusts – within your catchment area
- specialist trusts – within your field of charitable work.

This restricted information should then be typed on to A4 sheets in landscape format and presented under five columns, as follows:

- column 1 – trust name, address and correspondent
- column 2 – annual grant income
- column 3 – trustees in full, listed by name
- column 4 – objectives, briefly noted in up to 10 words
- column 5 – other special features, very briefly noted.

Now you are ready to meet your first helper and ask for assistance with personal introductions.

What type of helper do you need?

Major trusts

The type of person you will need to help you with introductions to major trusts is far from obvious to those who have not conducted a trust grants campaign. You would initially expect that a leading businessperson or an eminent technical specialist would be just the sort of supporter to secure the attention of a trust. The reality, however, is that it is friendship and not career success that is the key to good introductions. Professional eminence is altogether a secondary factor.

So how do you identify helpers with such an unspecific profile – the possible friends of listed, unknown trustees? The answer is that a good many of the trustees on your list will be far from the unknowns you suppose them to be.

Glance for a moment at your list of 50 major trusts. Whatever method you have used to compile this list, you will at once recognise that a significant proportion of the names qualify for the unofficial title 'The great and the good'. Here is a cross-section of that well-disposed and socially eminent group of people whose lives are quietly spent in discreet service to their country and community. Nowhere are these old-fashioned virtues better represented than on the boards of the leading grant-making trusts.

It now becomes clear what type of helpers you will need – they should be people who move in these distinguished circles. If you can find several helpers of this type then, between them, they will be able to identify contacts at many of the major trusts you have listed.

Local and specialist trusts

Local and specialist trusts are less likely to have distinguished people on their boards, although there are many exceptions to this general rule.

Evidently, to make introductions on the basis of friendship in these cases, further helpers will need to be found, whose lives interact with the trustees concerned – helpers who are socially active within a particular county or neighbourhood and who will assist you with local trusts. Where the trust specialises in your particular field of work, then you will need to recruit external helpers who are familiar with this area of charitable activity.

How do you recruit your helpers?

Major trusts

Faced with the unfamiliar task of recruiting distinguished helpers for your charitable approaches, your first reaction may be to hold your head in your hands. The chances of succeeding in this objective seem slender, even non-existent.

The problem is more imaginary than real, and the first point to note is that your task will have been made much easier if you have laid the groundwork for this recruitment before the recruitment drive itself is mounted. In a perfect world you will already have invited the Mayor, the Bishop, the Lord Lieutenant or other leaders to become patrons of your charity. Where such steps have been taken, then the business of finding further active, eminent helpers to make your trust approaches is greatly simplified. People will do much to support the causes that their local leaders have espoused.

Let us assume, however, that you are starting your helper recruitment from scratch, and that you have no honorary patrons who could attract them to your cause. We will also assume, for illustrative purposes, that your charity or your project is sited within a defined geographical area. Should that not be the case, then the basic principles of recruitment will need to be adapted to the circumstances, even if they will not fundamentally change.

People active in public life are often confident and fully aware of the role expected of them in making supportive introductions on behalf of a range of good causes. For the volunteer concerned, this often acts as an important element in cementing his or her own aspirations in relation to personal esteem and social cachet.

Given the fundraiser's ability to support the administrative and research functions associated with volunteer-led introductions, the task facing the volunteer will not be at all daunting. Indeed, it is hard to imagine any role that is capable of achieving so good an effect from so modest an outlay of valuable time. All that you will ask your helpers to do is to write a small number of introductory letters to acquaintances who happen to be the trustees of major trusts. There are no further duties – no committee meetings, minutes or action points beyond the simple, letter-writing task.

If you do not yet know which eminent people live within your area, then you have been working up to now in a vacuum of your own choosing. Nevertheless, a good social directory, such as *Debrett's People of Today* (available for subscription online at tinyurl.com/peopleoftodayonline) will supply the information you need.

Now write a letter

Your first letter, let us say, is to a local baronet, Sir Jasper Hackforth. You have not met Sir Jasper before, nor does he know of you. The letter you write to Sir Jasper will, of course, be courteous and, necessarily, rather long. In it you will summarise your work, stressing that he and you are near neighbours, and touching judiciously on the task that you have in mind for him. Spell out that, in helping you, he will not become entangled in your day-to-day concerns and administration. There will be no burdensome involvement other than the opening of one or two doors in the direction of grant-making trusts.

Sir Jasper may, of course, decline to assist you, but that is not the usual response. It is more likely that he will write back with friendly and genuine modesty:

'I should be happy to see you if you wish, although I am inclined to doubt whether I could be of any use. Nonetheless, if you feel that I may be of some help to you in your charitable work, do please give me a ring to see if we can find a moment to meet.'

So, your first helper has agreed to see you. The meeting you arrange should ideally be at Sir Jasper's house. This will cause as little disruption as possible to his normal day. Such considerations should be a constant feature of all your work with your distinguished helpers.

Local and specialist trusts

The same principles apply to recruiting local and specialist helpers: the same courtesies and the same care in using your supporters' time sparingly and to good effect.

For approaches to local and regional trusts, you can enlist the help of solicitors, accountants or estate agents who know the neighbourhood well.

For approaches to specialist trusts, your own knowledge of the field will normally suggest some well-disposed and widely respected advisers.

The meeting with the helper

There is nothing to be feared in a meeting with an eminent helper, or indeed with any helper. The fact that Sir Jasper has agreed to make time available is already proof of his kindly disposition towards you. Provided you have prepared yourself well and provided that you do not trespass too far on your helper's freely given time, your meeting will be successful.

In harmony with Sir Jasper's natural pace, therefore, you should discreetly move the business forward, aiming to engage his thoughts for no more than 45 minutes:

● First, re-cap on the work of your charity and on the purpose of your visit, so that Sir Jasper is reminded of your objectives.

● Second, hand Sir Jasper your project document for future reading. He may glance at this briefly and ask some simple questions.

● Third, hand Sir Jasper your list of major trusts and draw his attention to the names of the trustees.

● Fourth, as Sir Jasper comments on the list, make brief, rapid notes of his remarks on your own master copy. A digest of this information should be confirmed back to him later.

In most cases you will find that, starting from a standpoint of diffidence, Sir Jasper will soon become charmed to find that he does indeed recognise several of the names listed. He may even become intrigued and enthusiastic:

'Is that the father or is it the son? If it's the father, I could certainly drop him a line. I don't suppose you could find out, could you?'

Take a note of such points: they will be very important for the future.

By the time he has gone through the list of major trusts, Sir Jasper may have found, say, five acquaintances to whom he could write. If his interest remains high, then the list of livery companies may be handed to him, and subsequently also the other two lists. However, it is very important that you judge your helper's stamina wisely. The fun of spotting acquaintances on a list can soon become a chore if you persevere insensitively.

By the time the meeting ends, there are seven people whom Sir Jasper knows well. There are also three further possibilities on whom more research work needs to be done.

At this point it is important to relieve Sir Jasper of every possible burden, even though he may be keen to get down to his tasks straight away.

Undertake to draft the letters that he will sign. Send Sir Jasper a note of the meeting and reassure him that at this stage he need do nothing more than wait to hear from you with a summary of the next steps to be taken.

Follow-up on a meeting with a helper

Detailed and accurate follow-up is necessary after every meeting with a helper. The follow-up also needs to be succinct, identifying all the nuances in as few words as possible. Once a full panel of helpers is at work, the need for precision becomes even more important. Several helpers may know the same trustee, and it is essential that recommendations are not accidentally duplicated.

Immediately on return to your office, therefore, summarise your discussions in a letter to Sir Jasper. Where additional research is required, do this at once and include the results in the summary. Attach to the summary the letter of recommendation that you are now asking Sir Jasper to write to his acquaintances.

One sample letter will occasionally be sufficient. More frequently, however, several letters will have to be prepared, because in a number of cases there will be special circumstances to refer to.

There are some golden rules:

• Sir Jasper must write from his own home, on his own notepaper and, if possible, in his own hand. Everything that indicates personal effort will reinforce his message.

• Sir Jasper should write a short friend-to-friend letter, not a formal application. He may change the wording you have suggested just as he pleases, but you will find that he will normally follow your original text fairly closely.

• Sir Jasper must write to his trustee friend at home. Letters sent to business addresses, clubs or the House of Lords are less effective, although sometimes unavoidable.

• The tone and wording of the letter must be distinctly more heartfelt than your natural British reserve would at first suggest: 'For much of my life I have admired the work of this small group', and so on.

• The letter, though it is by no means a formal application, must close with a request that a formal application may be sent. 'All I would ask, Hector, is that my friends at this charity might prepare a formal application for the Knatchpole Trust to consider. Nothing would please me more than to have your encouragement for this to be done.'

The outcome of the helper's work

Friend-to-friend letters, although they work very well in the trust fund-raising field, cannot, of course, work every time. If the helper has written before, on several charitable themes, then the impact will be reduced. If the helper is more of a passing acquaintance than a friend, then that too will be reflected in the reply.

Finally, you must always remember that trust funds are under constant and increasing pressure. It may simply not be possible for trustees to make an award in some instances, however much they may wish to do so. At its best, however, the method described has the singular effect of bypassing the initial assessment stage in a trust's deliberations, thus ensuring a smooth passage of your case from the letter-box to the shortlist.

In response to Sir Jasper's recommendation, his friend Sir Hector Knatchpole replies:

> *Dear Jasper,*
>
> *Many thanks for your note about the Botswana Herons' Egg Society. We will certainly see if we can help. Funds are a bit stretched at present, but it does sound a most deserving cause. Do please ask your friends to write to our Correspondent, Marcus Protheroe, with a full application. We next meet in May.*
>
> *Yours ever,*
>
> *Hector.*

All now depends on the quality of the formal application itself.

References

Debrett's People of Today, Debrett's, 2010.

CHAPTER EIGHT
Making the application

Anthony Clay

Planning to avoid rejection

The key to avoiding rejection is to have done everything necessary before the final moment when you make the formal application. Whenever possible, the application should arrive after several previous communications have been held with the trust and should, ideally, reflect this earlier work.

Typically, an accompanying letter should be along the lines of: 'Following our previous conversations and your visit on 13 August we are now enclosing our formal application to the trustees who, we understand, are meeting on 22 October', possibly with a further paragraph of explanation. For example: 'You will see that the amount we are asking for is the sum needed to ensure that this project happens'.

Sometimes, it will not have been possible to go through all these preparations. The size of the trust's grants may be so small that the time and effort in preliminary work may not be justified. Many trusts simply refuse to engage in any discussions or preliminaries, insisting on a written application only.

Whatever earlier work you have been able to do, it is essential to follow the trust's rules and procedures to the letter.

The trust's requirements

The policies and application rules can be flexible or rigid, but frequently reflect the personalities of the trustees.

Examples of two very different trust guidelines

McClaren Foundation

(Objects include animal welfare, war disabled, regimental charities, refugees from communism, distressed widows and pensioners of the professional income group, general charitable purposes.)

Enjoyable expeditions overseas for students on the pretext of some scientific investigation of doubtful utility that claims to compress into two to three weeks' scientific work that will require a period of years, or to assist for a few weeks a native population to carry out simple construction works that they are far better able to carry out themselves are not entertained. The Trustees will use their best endeavours not to be prejudiced against an application that uses the jargon evolved by the new Welfare Industry such as "caring", "underprivileged" and "deprived".'

Christie Charitable Trust

(Objects are general charitable purposes and to promote medical research and education.)

'Assistance is given to special causes and charitable bodies of special interest to the Trustees. Appeals of the "expensive glossy brochure" variety are neither welcomed nor considered.'

Some trusts will be happy to let you have written instructions about what they require; others simply leave it up to you. Some have very detailed forms to complete; others ask only for a short letter. All of the larger trusts have websites, some of which are extremely helpful.

Deciding how much to ask for

This is a very difficult point. You should be primarily guided by the results of any research that you have been able to carry out into the trust's income and the money it has available for grant distribution.

Sometimes the published directories (for example, DSC's online subscription site www.trustfunding.org.uk) will give an indication of typical grant sizes and this can be helpful. The first rule must be dictated by the scale and timespan of the charity's need and the nature of the project to meet that need.

One rule of thumb is that you should ask for up to 10% of the trust's annual grants figure, but this can be misleading because much will depend upon how many grants are being made and their average size.

Occasionally, trusts may give away very large amounts of capital:

• benefactors may top up a trust to enable special grants to be made

• a trust may have received an extraordinary income in the previous year

• from time to time trusts are wound up altogether, sometimes distributing all the assets to one beneficiary.

It could be a sign of rather unhealthy thinking when grantseekers try to pool projects to reach the highest possible grant size that a trust has ever made. There should be much better matching of project to trust and vice versa. Never artificially raise the cost of a project to meet a higher grant-size opportunity.

The application itself

In 1998 *Third Sector* reported the *International Journal of Nonprofit and Voluntary Sector Marketing*, vol. 3, no. 2 to have shown the following:

Key mistakes by applicants to grant-making trusts of trusts identifying	%
Did not read requirements	55.3
Sent large amounts of unnecessary information	23.4
Application was very poorly presented	19.1
Did not state how funds would be used	14.9
Application was impersonal	12.8
Sent insufficient information for decision to be made	6.4
Application was too 'plush'	6.4

Although to many people who are inexperienced in trust fundraising the application may seem the key element in the process, what really matters is what has preceded the application. Nevertheless there are several important points to remember:

• Always follow the trust's instructions.

• Do not make handwritten applications unless they are beautifully legible.

• Be clear and precise.

• Answer all the key questions, such as who will benefit, how the project will be evaluated, what other funding you are getting.

• Make sure the application arrives on time. Send it by special delivery if necessary.

Notes to applicants from a trust administrator

(With grateful thanks to Clive Marks of the Lord Ashdown Charitable Trust)

Five ideas for the waste-paper basket

- The blanket appeal
- Dear Sir/Madam
- Very glossy
- Shock tactics – 'exciting', 'unique', 'desperate', 'exciting new challenge', 'unless you help, he/she will die'
- Undated

Size and appearance

- One to two sides A4, typed
- Come to the point quickly
- An appropriate photograph
- No jargon – good English, no acronyms
- Get someone to 'play devil's advocate' when the application is complete

Five ideas for the content

- Say who else is helping you
- What you completed last year – what has to be done now
- The size of your organisation – the number of paid staff and volunteers
- Numbers of people helped
- Newspaper cuttings

The figure

This is the most difficult part of the letter

- It must come early on
- Be specific

- If very large don't write until a personal contact is made on a trustee-to-trustee basis

- If you are raising £500,000 for building or equipment, explain how you intend to maintain that asset in future years

CHAPTER NINE

Applications: a trust's view

Des Palmer

These dos and don'ts were first written some years ago, after extensive input from half a dozen of the country's most open and active trusts. They have been updated for this new edition after feedback from current practitioners, especially Bharat Mehta, CEO of Trust for London.

What to do; what not to do

Applying to charitable trusts can be something of a lottery. There is no perfect way, there is no formula, no magic phrase, that guarantees success; it is an exercise that in some ways is as much a gamble as picking a set of National Lottery numbers. Many grantseekers appear to think otherwise and regularly asked the staff of Allied Dunbar's Community Affairs Department for advice on how best to approach charitable trusts. Our guidance was written partly to show that there is no one golden key but also to make available what few guidelines do exist so that both grant-seekers and grantgivers might benefit: the former by expending less effort and becoming more effective, the latter by having fewer inappropriate applications to deal with.

After many years' experience of managing the four Allied Dunbar grant-giving funds, we developed a fairly good idea as to what constitutes a good or a bad application. However, we felt that our case would be supported if we sought the views of our peers, some of whom are infinitely more experienced and wiser than we are. From their responses we fashioned a list of 'dos' and 'don'ts', using their exact words wherever possible.

A few words on the grant-giving trust world

The grant-giving trust world has some truly outstanding trusts, managed by wise and imaginative trustees and capable and objective trust administrators. However, the overall picture is more generally of cautious and unimaginative trustees, and volunteer, or hard-pressed part-time paid, administrators.

The overwhelming majority of trusts are run by volunteers. By that I mean there are no paid part-time, let alone full-time, staff to open mail, read applications, sort them out, reject the majority, seek information on a few, travel hundreds of miles to visit, write reports, prepare agendas, organise meetings, write minutes, send rejection letters, send letters announcing success, write and send cheques, monitor and report back on grants, prepare annual reports, fill in innumerable questionnaires, answer the telephone, and so on. Even when there are staff, they are invariably hard-pressed and often face a deluge of applications. The responses to applications will therefore vary considerably.

The 'dos' of applying

The 'dos' divide themselves into four sections: preliminary work, the general principles of an application, the specific detail required in an application and what to do afterwards.

Preliminary work

● Think ahead. Work out your organisation's income and expenditure, not just for this year but for next year, and even the year after. All fundraising takes time; if you want to avoid financial crises, plan well ahead.

● Research the trusts – find out their funding programme and geographical interests. Where possible, find out the names of officers and where to write. Try to use up-to-date directories (eight years after changing our name, we still received letters addressed to the Hambro Life Charitable Trust).

● Find out, by using the directories, your local charities information bureau, Citizens' Advice office or from other grantseekers, how each trust prefers to be approached – some encourage informal telephone calls, while for others this would be the fastest road to rejection.

● You must be clear about what you want and why you want it, and you must find out as much as you can about the trusts you are planning to approach.

● Our in-tray was full of misdirected applications: this was a waste of our time, but it has also wasted your time if, by applying in this way, you do not stand a chance. There is little point, indeed there is no point at all, in a youth club in the western corner of Wiltshire applying to a trust whose only aim is to 'alleviate poverty among former school teachers in Yorkshire'.

● Always check the web for up-to-date information about the trusts to which you are applying. All the major givers now have websites and some are very helpful. A trust that has spent time and money on developing a website will not be pleased if your application demonstrates that you have not looked at it carefully enough.

The general principles of an application

Make sure that your application is:

- **Concise.** On the back windows of cars you can see slogans advertising the driver's peccadilloes such as 'Windsurfers do it standing up'. A vicar friend of ours had on the back of his jogging vest 'Vicars do it on their knees'. Trusts' administrators have engraved on their hearts 'Grant administrators like it done on two sides of A4'.

- **Attractively presented,** but not so flash as to ring alarm bells about profligate spending on fundraising.

- **On time.** 'Sorry I can't make your deadline: the typist is sick/headquarters haven't sent the accounts/the chair is on holiday, etc.' Trust administrators set deadlines not because they are training for a career in the civil service but because they have a timetable to keep to. It is the trustees who decide which applications to support at meetings that may be held once a year, once a quarter or once a month. A trust administrator needs sufficient time to assemble applications, draw up agendas and circulate paper.

- **Addressed to the right person,** with the name and address correctly spelt. Joel Joffe, former chair of the Allied Dunbar Charitable Trust, has been addressed as Noel, Toffe, Coffee and Joff. I, Des Palmer, simply hate to be addressed as Des Wilson. Jerry Marston still reacts very badly to being mistaken on paper for an ageing Merseyside pop singer.

- **Appropriate to that particular trust,** in terms of both its declared policies and the size of grant you ask for. Don't ask for £90,000 from a trust whose largest grant is normally only £3,000 or which only has £3,000 to give away.

The application – specific details

Each application should include:

- a short, general description of your organisation

- a specific description of the project or part of the organisation for which you are looking for funds, and what you are hoping to achieve.

These objectives should be clear and realistic. If the prospective grantmaker has funding priorities, state how your work fits them:

• specific information about the nature and the size of the need or problem that you are attempting to address. Avoid broad generalisations such as 'addressing the needs of older people in Warminster', or 'there is a desperate need for the service we plan to provide'

• the cost of the project (or item) with, where necessary, a realistic, itemised budget for the work in question. It still amazes administrators when they receive applications that give no indication as to whether the cost in question is £5, £500, £5,000 or £500,000

• the project's timescale: when you plan to start and how long the project will run

• information as to whether other funders have been approached: are any applications under consideration and have any grants been given?

• an indication, if a long-term project, of the possible sources of ongoing funding after the grant-aid applied for has finished

• some indication of how you intend to evaluate your project (how will you measure success?)

• the latest set of accounts and an annual report. Bear in mind, however, that supporting material is not usually seen by the trustees and often will have to be condensed into no more than a paragraph or two

• the name, status, email address and telephone number of a contact person

• your registered charity number, if relevant

• send the application in the manner requested – some funders like electronic versions only, others prefer hard copies, some may want both.

Afterwards

In many activities in life, once gratified, our initial eagerness to please changes to indifference or forgetfulness. It is important to acknowledge receipt of a grant and to send back appropriately completed and signed agreements if that is what is required. Do so within the timescales stated in the offer letter. Always say thank you – you may want to reapply to that particular trust in a year or two's time: whatever other qualities trust administrators may lack, they mostly have memories like the proverbial elephant.

Make a note of any requests or requirements for further information and ensure that you respond accordingly. It is also worth keeping in touch, telling the grantgiver about your progress, highlighting your success, inviting trustees to see your project on a special day or specific time. Building a relationship that is based upon respect on both sides is not possible with all trusts, but it is certainly worthwhile putting in the effort. Trustees like to fund success: that is why they are in business. A satisfied trustee or administrator is more likely to want to consider further support.

The 'do nots'

Do not:

• submit too much material or be verbose. A page and a half should be the absolute maximum for most projects: less if you can manage it

• submit out-of-date material

• use jargon (nobody but you will understand it)

• send a handwritten appeal (these are difficult to read)

• send a duplicated mailshot (straight in the waste-paper basket)

• answer questions on a standard application form with 'see attached'

• apply pressure by alluding to meetings or chance encounters with trustees 'who have encouraged me to write to you'

• end a letter with 'I would like this appeal to be taken seriously' (a guaranteed turn-off)

• respond to a rejection letter by sending an angry, rude or an insulting reply. A number of trusts have complaints procedures. Rarely are they procedures for complaints against decisions already taken.

Some final thoughts

These may not be the pearls of wisdom that you had expected to drip from our collective silver pens. It is, perhaps you are saying, nothing but 'common sense'.

We made no claims at the beginning to provide you with keys to the saferoom doors. Fundraising is time consuming, and hard work, requiring patience, tenacity and a dose of good fortune. Trusts vary greatly, and there is no single formula that will guarantee success.

There is no one absolute model application but there are plenty of ways of making a good one into a bad one.

PART FOUR

Maintaining Effective Relationships

CHAPTER TEN

Acknowledgement, recognition and reporting

David Saint

Introduction

Phew! After perhaps weeks of work, the trust application is placed in the post tray, or submitted electronically, for safe delivery to your prospective donor. Thank goodness that's over!

Unfortunately, it is not. If you are serious about securing a grant, rather than simply 'going through the process', there is much more you can and should do to ensure success – this time or next.

It is important to bear in mind the fact that there *will be* a next time. A few trusts almost always turn down the first application from a charity to see just how serious it is, and how the charity conducts itself. The steps you take once you have sent in your application could influence the decision about that grant, and future ones.

Keeping track of progress

You may have applied to a number of trusts. Perhaps you are also responsible for approaches to other types of funder. It can be very easy to lose touch with the progress of an application.

Does this matter? Often not, perhaps, but if the grant is important to you it will be worth taking a few extra steps to increase the likelihood of success.

The way in which you record progress will depend upon how you normally do things – the system has to be comfortable or it will not be used. It should, however, contain three elements:

- First, a filing system will be essential, to enable you quickly to retrieve all the papers relating to a particular prospect as required. This may be electronic and/or a hard copy.

- The second element is a simple checklist of all the necessary actions, when they should be taken, and by whom.

- Finally, a diary function will be invaluable, to ensure that those actions are taken at the right time, without undue haste or panic.

It will be crucial to refer to the diary function on a daily basis (so it helps if this is an actual diary and/or an electronic prompt) to ensure that the system works. If the system is used for a large number of applications or for other project management purposes as well, it makes a lot more sense and using becomes second nature.

Keeping trusts informed

It is as dangerous to generalise about relationships with trusts as it is to generalise about relationships with people. However, when we recognise that trust fundraising has a lot to do with building relationships with the people making the grants, it becomes easier to understand what might be required.

Relationships are all about communication – but relevant communication. Trusts will generally welcome information about your project if it has a bearing on your application. Success in obtaining partial funding from a different source, a material alteration in the project team or the project itself, an award or achievement that reinforces your organisation's ability to deliver the project – all these things will be relevant to a potential funder and should be brought to the trust's attention. Simply bombarding a funder with newsletters or, worse still, direct mail appeals, will not be helpful.

Sometimes it will be sufficient to telephone the correspondent to advise him or her of the new information. In other circumstances a simple letter will suffice. If the change is significant your application may have to be rewritten or even withdrawn. Funders will generally respect an applicant who takes a responsible attitude to the information supplied. They may be less impressed by one that simply seems unable to make up its mind.

Following acknowledgement requirements

Many trusts have specific preferences when it comes to acknowledgement of grants. Some wish to remain anonymous, perhaps because of their ethos of giving, or to avoid an avalanche of similar applications. It can be tempting to let the name slip, particularly in support of an application to another funder, but this should only be done with the express written permission of the donor.

Some trusts request an acknowledgement in the charity's annual report. If so, do not simply make the acknowledgement – remember to send a copy to the donor, stating in the covering letter the page on which the acknowledgement can be found. Make sure (at proof stage) that the donor's name has been spelled correctly.

Occasionally a trust will ask for a more overt acknowledgement, particularly in respect of larger grants. This could be anything from a plaque on a piece of furniture to the naming of a building. Discuss with the trust the precise requirements and their implications (for example the cost to the charity of providing the acknowledgement, or the feelings of other, perhaps larger, donors). When the requirements have been agreed, be sure they are implemented in good time and that the trust is invited to send a representative to see the project and the acknowledgement, or perhaps is sent a photograph of it.

Remember that if trusts have rules (perhaps forming part of their trust deed) they will expect those rules to be followed. You may flout them once and get away with it. Any future application is very unlikely to be successful.

Thanking trusts

The other important thing to remember about trusts is that they are administered by people. Thanking trusts needs to work at two, or possibly three, levels.

The first level we have already considered – the public acknowledgement (or not) requested by the trust.

The second level is the formal thank-you letter. One should always be sent, but this is frequently overlooked. Send one. The letter should be neither overly effusive nor a terse two-liner. It should be a personal letter addressed to the person who wrote the letter confirming the grant or the person who signed the cheque, thanking the trust and the trustees for the grant of (amount) for (project). It may be appropriate to add a little information on the project that did not appear in the original application, or to say something about the specific impact that the grant will have. It can also be worth mentioning in passing any other work you are doing that may be of interest to the trust in the future, but *do not* ask for a further grant at this stage.

If there is an opportunity to go to a third level of thanks, this can be highly beneficial. The correspondent or one of the trustees may have been very helpful to you in the application process or instrumental in securing a positive decision. Such input usually goes unnoticed and unacknowledged, especially if it is by a staff member, but expressing thanks person-to-person helps to build an important relationship which is not only good in its own right, it also lays first class foundations for subsequent applications.

Reporting on progress

The process should not even end with the thank yous. With the possible exception of smaller grants for one-off items, it can be valuable to update trusts from time to time on the way your project is unfolding. Again this should not be in the form of junk mail (although update sheets that receive a wider circulation may be appropriate). The frequency of these reports will be determined by any criteria set by the trust, the duration of the project, and perhaps the size of the grant. Updates should only be sent when there is some news (even if this is bad), and not so frequently that the trust is inundated with paper or emails. A grant to cover a year's project might warrant two or three updates; a three-month project might justify a report halfway through and at the end.

Keeping the trust involved

The staff and/or trustees of most trusts will simply not have the time to do anything much more than receive your reports – and perhaps only to skim read them. Others, however, will take a much more hands-on approach to their grantmaking and may wish to become quite involved in the project. In the case of substantial grants the trust may want to have a nominee on your management committee or equivalent. In other cases the trust may simply want to attend occasional meetings or visit the project from time to time. It is possible that the active involvement of a trust representative may be (or seem to be) unwelcome interference. It is more likely that other significant benefits will flow. The trust and its representative will be anxious to ensure that its grant is effective, and will wish to offer help and advice to ensure that the project succeeds. Their experience and expertise may complement your own; their contacts and influence may be very important to you. On the whole, the direct involvement of a trust representative can be highly beneficial, and should be encouraged if it seems possible.

Following up

Following up applies in every circumstance. The nature and timing of that follow-up will vary from situation to situation.

• **The trust informs you your project is outside its terms of reference.** If your research is at fault there is not much you can do. A short, courteous letter of apology for taking up the trust's time would not go amiss. If the published information suggests your project *should* be of interest to the trust, phone or write to request current guidelines, or clarification of them, if you already have a copy.

• **The trust advises you that its funds are fully committed.** If not revealed in the rest of the letter, phone or write to find out whether this will be the case for the foreseeable *future* and, if not, whether in principle your project is of interest and when you should reapply.

- **The trust invites you to reapply.** Do so, when it suggests, providing any further information requested.

- **The trust offers a grant but does not enclose payment.** Carry out any action requested, such as advising the trust when work on the project has begun. Make a diary note to do this if it cannot be done immediately. If you do not receive payment within a reasonable period of a grant being approved (say four weeks) inquire politely whether it has been sent. Mistakes can happen – at either end.

- **The grant is received.** Acknowledge it, as outlined on page 79. Read any accompanying material carefully, and ensure that you comply with any requirements stated. If circumstances have changed so much that you will not be able to spend the grant for the purpose stated in your application (perhaps the project has been fully funded from elsewhere, or that precise activity is no longer needed), do not hesitate to return the money. Although this will be a painful thing to do after all the effort you made to get it, you have a legal obligation to do this if you are not going to spend it as the donor expects. Of at least equal importance is the fact that this will earn you the considerable respect of the trust, and may ease significantly other dealings you may have with it.

- **The period or project that a grant is to cover has elapsed.** By this time the project will probably be very low on your list of priorities. It has been around a long time, other matters will have become more urgent or important, and new initiatives will be clamouring for your fundraising attention. Do not be beguiled by them! Use your diary system to remind you to send a final report on the project to the trust(s) (and other major donor(s)) that supported it – whether or not this was a condition of the grant. This is not only courteous, but also helps develop good relationships on which to found your next application.

- **A year has gone by.** Unless a trust states otherwise, it is generally felt that 12 months should elapse between applications. Do not make this rigid, so that your applications become mechanistic and predictable, but do not assume that if you have received one grant you will be unlikely to be favoured again for some time. The reverse is often the case, especially if you have been sensible and conscientious in your acknowledgement, recognition and reporting.

CHAPTER ELEVEN

Consolidation

Roger Mitty

Introduction

Often, we hear experienced fundraisers declare that fundraising is a people business and that 'people give to people'. Although true, this philosophy should not be reserved exclusively for fundraising from individuals. Other fundraising methodologies, whether they involve companies, organisations or trusts, still involve people. Grants received by charities from grant-making trusts are essentially the result of people (in the form of administrators and trustees) responding to people (representing charitable organisations) and what they seek to provide for the constituency or cause they seek to serve.

The application is not the final act

It is important to understand that an application to a grant-making trust, whether or not successful, should not be seen as the end of a process. It should always been seen as either the beginning or the continuation of a potentially fruitful relationship between two organisations.

Information recording

This section addresses the need for, and covers the detail of, effective recording systems. Such systems will play a vital part in supporting and driving the ongoing communications process a charity uses to consolidate its relationship with an individual trust. It is very important to keep detailed and up-to-date records of the results of your organisation's applications to grant-making trusts, whatever their outcome.

This kind of information gathering is, of course, an ongoing process. This data, a combination of a charity's initial and ongoing research, will form the basis of an increasingly comprehensive database on all of those trusts whose objects are in line with your particular cause.

This information resource will become the single, most valuable asset to support the delivery of your researched and carefully phased strategy for fundraising from grant-making trusts and foundations.

Organisations are constantly evolving. In the same way, charities will regularly reappraise their priorities, the relevance of their work and ways in which they need to adapt to meet increasing or changing needs. As well as recording all trust applications, new projects and new areas of work need to be recorded centrally. All areas of work should be regularly evaluated in terms of their relevance to the existing portfolio of trusts and their urgency. There may also be other factors, for example working in new geographical areas, that will also affect the way a charity needs to adapt its fundraising strategy.

Keeping up with change

One of the single most important new developments that will affect trust fundraising will be when a charity moves into an area of operation beyond its traditional activities. It is almost certain that such changes will open up opportunities to consider an approach to a whole new tranche of trusts whose objects cover the new initiatives.

Ongoing communication

Good trust fundraisers will grasp every opportunity to foster ongoing communications and a relationship with all of the trusts in which their charity is interested. This means identifying each trust's key voluntary or paid staff and ensuring effective and appropriate communications with them. This may involve providing annual reports and/or ongoing updates on the charity's work or, even more importantly, the occasional invitation to trust representatives to visit projects in which they might have a particular interest. Occasionally trustees or trust representatives should be invited to functions where the aim is to cultivate the interest of potential donors or thank those who have given, either when a trust-funded project has been completed or when other friends or supporters, including other trusts, are gathered to hear from the charity leadership about its successes and vision.

Sometimes individual trustees will want to visit a project or meet relevant representatives of a charity as part of the application process. Again it is important to keep a thorough record of those visits and refer to them in ongoing communications with the trust.

In any active trust fundraising programme there will probably be a substantial number of trusts that have not responded to applications or eventually decline a grant. As with all areas of modern fundraising, increasing numbers of organisations are approaching trusts and foundations and so the chances of success will be reduced. This reinforces the need for a properly researched and phased strategic approach to the process and the importance of building good communications and nurturing relationships.

Just because a trust has rejected an application on one occasion does not mean that a charity should not reapply. Further approaches will often be worthwhile, especially if they are for a different type of project or proposition.

Because of the increasing number of applications trusts are sometimes reluctant to enter into any kind of communication with fundraising organisations or discuss reasons for the failure of a particular application. However, it may be worthwhile for the charity to try to establish whether a trust is prepared to discuss why a particular application has failed and give guidance and even encouragement about future applications.

To communicate effectively with a trust it is important to establish who the individual trustees are and therefore the type of ongoing information and communication they will welcome. For example, they may be medical experts, accountants or lawyers, all of whom may have different kinds of needs and interests in a particular charity's work.

The purpose of the consolidation phase is to enable the development of committed and increasing support for the charity from grant-making trusts. As the organisation establishes a regular programme of trust fundraising there are a number of key areas that will need attention as part of the consolidation process.

Research

No organisation can ever know too much about a potential source of funds and far too many fundraising organisations attempt to engage in specific fundraising activity with too little information and understanding about the individual or organisation from which they seek support. Research always has an important role: it is often said that 50% of all fundraising activity should focus on research. A full understanding of how trusts and foundations operate and a continuing and ongoing research process are essential. A charity needs to identify new trusts as well as changes in existing trusts' trustees, personnel or objects. Changes in trusts' objects and trustees and/or their personal preferences and the way they interpret and apply the objects are more common than many people realise. Sometimes those changes can be quite dramatic and fundraisers must always be vigilant and do all they can to be aware of them.

Contacts

Most people who are experienced in fundraising from trusts will appreciate that a charity should get its application in through any route except the letter box, if at all possible. The chapter began by talking about fundraising as a 'people' business and saying that 'people give to people'. Because of this, the ability to identify and use personal contacts in developing your communications with grant-making trusts cannot be over-emphasised. The charity will need to have in place a research process to utilise the knowledge of any new committee members, trustees, friends and even supporters who become more closely involved and engaged with the charity and its work and vision.

There are countless experiences that demonstrate that when a charity is able to make personal contact with a trustee and create and encourage opportunities for face-to-face conversations to encourage an interest in their organisation, the chances of a successful application are substantially increased. It is also the case that trust representatives are often willing to talk to charities considering an application. They appreciate and respond positively to organisations that have taken the time and the trouble to conduct quality research and therefore can speak knowledgeably about individual trusts to their representatives. Such personal contact also provides an opportunity for fundraisers to hear what the trust is looking for. Sometimes, in their enthusiasm to grasp an opportunity to present the urgency of their cause, fundraisers miss an opportunity to understand the prospective donor's views and needs. Whenever a representative of a charity makes personal contact with a trust representative, be that an administrator or trustee, there should be a full debrief of that individual in order that he or she can provide feedback to assist in the application process.

Application intervals

Understandably many grant-making trusts will only accept an application from an individual charity once a year. Some trusts state when the next application can be made and occasionally charities may be able to approach a particular trust more than once in a year if there is a one-off or urgent need. Conversely, there are other trusts that require a three-year or even longer interval between applications, wishing to be only occasional supporters. Because of this, charities will need to regularly monitor individual trusts' application intervals. This is of course much easier if the charity is engaging in a structured communications process and relation-ship building activity rather than simply sending applications at random through the post. It is worth remembering that this policy may also change as a trust grows, shrinks or appoints different administrative or trustee personnel.

Lead times

The time between the submission of a grant application and final con-sideration of that application by trustees, and the process by which the charity is informed will vary tremendously from trust to trust. As an example, those lead times may vary from a few weeks for some smaller trusts to over a year for the much larger and more popular trusts. It is the fundraiser's responsibility to research and understand the process on an individual trust basis and keep the organisation informed of these processes. Charities are always conscious of cash flow and expectations may be unrealistic if a charity's senior representatives expect that an application to a trust means a response and money in the bank within weeks!

Evaluating success

A great deal can be learnt from careful evaluation of the success or otherwise of presenting different types of projects or engaging in different styles of approach to grant-making trusts. It is therefore important to monitor carefully your charity's success (or otherwise) in meeting financial targets for trusts fundraising. Keeping track of responses from trusts to other charities, for example by examining trusts' grant lists in favour of charities similar to yours, may give a valuable insight into your charity's own success.

Gap analysis

There is every indication that the fundraising environment will continue to become increasingly competitive. Like most organisations, charities and other not-for-profit organisations are constantly changing. Charities introduce new projects and new services, and expand into new geographical areas. There are also constant changes in how trusts operate and how trustees address the considerable responsibility of distributing their trusts' funds. Every month new trusts are established. Sometimes these new trusts are unwilling to advertise their presence widely for fear of being over-whelmed with applications. Fundraisers need to ensure that they are doing all that is reasonably possible to identify these changes, recognise new opportunities and adapt their approaches to optimise success rates.

Summary

Good planning and research are essential to fundraising success. Successful trust fundraisers' results clearly demonstrate that the extra efforts applied to planning, organising and consolidating in the ways described in this book are worthwhile, even for the smallest of charities. It is disappointing that so many fundraising organisations are still not prepared to invest sufficiently in an area of opportunity that will continue to make millions of pounds available to the charity sector.

By rigorously following a strategic and phased approach to fund-raising from trusts and foundations, fundraisers have an opportunity to attract a steady stream of income to their cause.

In consolidating their success at the very least charities should always:

- record results

- report regularly, appropriately and personally to trusts on the progress of projects those trusts have supported and, indeed, other projects that fall within their area of interest

- develop a regular programme of contact, including visits by trust representatives to projects

- continue a process of research on existing and new trusts

- carefully monitor lead times for applications

- regularly evaluate relative success across projects and application styles

- report application results to the organisation as a whole, including your volunteers

- coordinate trust fundraising activity with other fundraising efforts

- frequently analyse research and look for new opportunities.

CHAPTER TWELVE

Recording systems

Peter Flory

Introduction

If you are going to use computers to help you monitor the process of fundraising from trusts, as I recommend that you do, and to carry out some of the mundane tasks involved, then you must ensure that you:

- record the right data at the right time
- have fast and efficient access to the data when you need it
- can produce letters and analysis reports at any time.

Key data to be used

You need to record the following types of data:

- basic trust details, including giving policy and procedures
- trustees and other contacts
- past and future actions
- applications made
- grants received
- thank-you letters and other general mailing history
- log of other communications
- funds/projects for which you need funds
- ad hoc notes.

Basic trust details

There are two types of information required here: standard contact data needed on any fundraising source and specific data required on trusts.

Standard data

This includes items such as:

- trust name
- address with separately identifiable fields for address lines: number/name, street, town, county and postcode
- telephone/fax numbers/email addresses
- name and job title of main trust contact
- name and job title of other trust contacts
- types of mailings/communications the contact should receive.

Specific data for a trust

This includes items such as:

- giving policy, including what they will/won't fund, which areas of the country/world they will/won't support, the frequency with which they will consider applications, for example don't apply again for three years
- application procedures
- when to apply, meeting dates and decision timetable
- total annual grants awarded for the last three years
- largest known single award
- average award
- who else they give to.

Trustees and other contacts

It is also essential to record details of individuals on the database and link them to any trusts or trustees they may know (with a two-way link) so that when viewing the trust record you can see a list of people and their relationship to the trust, for example trustee, chief executive, administrator, and, conversely, when viewing an individual's record you can see the organisations (and other people) with which/whom they have a relationship, and the nature of that relationship.

Past and future actions

This is a simple record consisting of date, action type (telephone call, letter, meeting, etc.), who created the action, to whom the action is assigned and an action summary/comment. A key useful feature here is to allow future dates to be entered and to have the actions automatically displayed on the computer screen on the appropriate day to remind you (or the person to whom you have assigned the action) of what you have to do today or this week.

Applications made

The application may be a simple letter or a complex proposal, but it is important to record the basics of each application such as:

- trust

- application date

- amount applied for

- what it was for (fund/project code)

- who is dealing with it

- status

- the amount awarded (and an automatic calculation of the award as a percentage of the application).

Grants received

When an award is made it is vital to record the amount received on the same record as the amount applied for, to carry out analysis. If you also have a standard format for recording all fundraising income the amount received must also be recorded there. This income record usually consists of:

- date

- supporter/donor (in this case, the trust) number

- amount

- campaign/appeal code (often a general code for trust applications)

- fund/project code (what the application was for)

- payment type

- payment method
- receipt indicator.

Thank-you letters and other general mailing history

This is a record created whenever any correspondence is sent to the trust, whether it is a standard thank-you letter, an application letter, a standard mailing or an ad hoc letter. It consists of date, letter type, who sent/signed it and a comment, and campaign/appeal and fund codes if relevant. Ideally this should also have a link to the text of the letter. This is for letters sent out to the trusts, but the concept can be extended to letters coming into your organisation. Some charities now scan incoming letters and link the scanned image to the trust, with a record similar to that outlined above.

Log of other communications

It helps to have a complete picture of all contacts with a trust and details of other communications with them, e.g. telephone calls (in and out), fax, email, meetings with them, events, etc., and details of trustees or trust staff who were invited to attend. These could all be included in a single Communication/Activity log with the letter details outlined in the previous paragraph.

Funds/projects

This is a record for every fund/project for which money is being sought. In its simplest form it contains a fund code, description, amount required, amount received to-date (which should be updated automatically as money is received).

Ad hoc notes

There will always be matters that should be recorded about a trust that do not fit into neat compartments, so an unlimited Notepad is an essential item. This should include the ability to date and timestamp each note and record who made it.

Key functions to be performed

All the functions required on the data described above are the same as those that you should expect of any contact database. They include the ability to easily:

- add and amend trust records and make maximum use of techniques such as picking items from drop-down lists, giving, for example, policy and action types

- add and amend applications

- add and amend details of mailings to, and other communications with, the trust

- link all trustees and other people you know at the trust to the trust record

- select trust records to view on screen immediately by inputting one or a combination of data items, for example trust name, trustee name, postcode or other elements of the address, geographic area served, particular giving policy

- carry out complex selections for mailing, for example all trusts that haven't given before which are based in the South East, or all trusts with a trustee who is also a personal donor to the charity

- use the output of selections to produce mail-merged letters or labels via a link with Microsoft Word and to produce mailing history records

- perform diary management, including an automatic reminder of due dates

- record other contacts, such as ad hoc letters and telephone calls

- record grants received, maintain every income item received against the respective trust and keep summary information for every trust, for example size of the first and last gift, the largest gift, the average gift value, the lifetime gift value and the total number of gifts

- run, as required, a set of standard reports including: number and value of applications made, awards received and success rate, specified time periods for applications that have been exceeded and amounts received year-to-date compared with budget

- carry out variable analyses of applications and income, for example by using an easy-to-use report writer within your database

- import names and addresses

- export data to other systems, for example spreadsheets, for further analysis and to produce graphical output.

Types of systems

There are two types of systems to consider:

• **Information directories available on CD-ROM or online.** These are invaluable sources of readily available information on trusts and they can even do some of the things one would normally associate with a contacts database, for example select a number of trusts in which you are interested, link them to a word-processing system and produce a mail-merged letter to them all (not a process recommended in trust fundraising). However, these directories are not the focus of this part of the book and they are best used in conjunction with a database (see next bullet) to provide the starting point for the application process.

• **One of the many packaged contact database/fundraising systems on the market (increasingly being called CRM, customer relationship management, systems).** There are at least 60 available, but it is fair to say that there are about a dozen market leaders, for example Raiser's Edge or thankQ. Most of these systems will have the facilities required to monitor the application process.

Why systems fail

Systems to help trust fundraisers fail to live up to their expectations and fall into disuse for a number of well-documented reasons:

• **The system is unfriendly and difficult to use** – no one is going to use a system to change a record and link to word processing to print letters or labels when it is quicker to amend an index card and type letters or labels in Word.

• **The data can be entered into the system but reporting it is difficult** – often to the extent that it is impossible to obtain the reports needed.

• **Inappropriate software** – the system doesn't do what you want it to do; in other words, it was specified incorrectly in the first place. Often these are bespoke systems (usually developed in Microsoft Access) for which there is no longer any in-house support.

• **Some systems are inflexible** – once the basic tables are set up they cannot be altered by users. Fundraising changes and flexibility is important. Neither the time nor the money is available to get information technology people to change the system.

• **Users do not keep the systems up to date** (often because the systems are so difficult to use). There is no point in entering all the trustees for a trust and linking all the records if it is not possible to keep up with changes and link new trustees and unlink ex-trustees as the changes occur.

• **The wrong details are recorded or the system does not allow the necessary data to be recorded.** This can lead to applications for the wrong things, such as asking for money for projects that the trust does not support, or asking for inappropriate amounts, for example £50,000 when the maximum grant is £5,000, or at the wrong time – applying in December when the trust allocates its grants in November.

• **Many systems are simply reactive data recorders rather than being proactive tools to help the fundraising process.** For example, recording historic actions is reactive but recording future actions and having the computer produce reminders on the appropriate day is proactive. A good system needs to be both.

• **Some systems link to word processing to send letters but do not automatically create a mailing history record** – so at a later date it is not possible to find out what was sent to whom.

Basic data requirements

• All identified trusts

• Those thoughtfully discounted, with reasons

• History of giving

• History of relationships

• Records of contacts

• Records of applications, successes, failures and rejections, with reasons

• Timespans for future action

• Built-in prompts

• All productive relationships

Avoiding failure

To avoid the installation of an inappropriate system, follow these golden rules for the selection of any piece of software:

• Set your objectives and be sure of what you are trying to achieve by installing the system.

• Define your requirements carefully and get the agreement of all interested parties.

• Allocate priorities to requirements – no system will do everything you can think of.

• Define selection criteria so that you have a benchmark for the comparison of competing systems.

• Check suppliers carefully, obtain proposals, see demonstrations and take up references.

• Ensure that someone understands the technical issues and can solve minor problems.

• Keep the data in the system up-to-date continually.

• Ensure all data in the system is accurate – remember GIGO (garbage in, garbage out)!

• Record all relevant data.

• Always set review dates.

• Track trustee movements.

• Record trustee interests.

PART FIVE

Additional Perspectives

CHAPTER THIRTEEN

The trust's perspective: applying to a charitable trust or foundation

The Association of Charitable Foundations (ACF)

Introduction

There are about 9,000 grant-making trusts and foundations in the UK, giving in total about £3.36 billion in grants to charitable causes each year (trustfunding.org.uk, DSC, 2010). This represents about 10% of the UK voluntary and community sector's income, similar in total to central government or local government. However, the government's statistical definition of 'voluntary and community' includes universities. When they are removed from the mix the figure is nearer 7 to 8%. The income from trusts and foundations to the voluntary and community sector is crucial to the sector's growth and to the development of a thriving civil society.

Grant-making trusts have a greater degree of independence than almost any other sector or funder. They are extremely diverse – not only in the scale and number of grants made and the type of trust but, in their age, style of grantmaking and the areas they support. A small but growing number of trusts are looking at ways in which they can offer support in addition to making grants, for example by offering loans or through advice on issues such as governance or other aspects of successfully running a charity.

What is a grant-making trust?

Most grant-making trusts and foundations derive their income from an endowment: a capital sum given to them by an individual, family or company. The endowment may take the form of cash, stocks, shares or land. It provides a tax-exempt income which funds the grantgiving. Some trusts and foundations receive their income from other sources, such as gifts from a company's current profits or a regular appeal on TV and radio. Some trusts act as a broker for donors and collector of endowment, in either a local area (a community foundation) or a specialist field (an intermediary trust).

What trusts fund

Because grant-making trusts are often privately endowed and therefore not reliant on either short-term popularity or government funding they are able to be creative, flexible and sometimes unorthodox in the use of their funds, and to take risks that other funders – in particular statutory bodies – are constrained from taking. Although trusts contribute a relatively modest proportion of total voluntary sector income, this contribution is very significant, especially when it comes to funding innovative ideas or areas of the sector that lack popular or political support.

Trusts like to concentrate their funding on:

- new methods of tackling problems

- disadvantaged and minority groups which have trouble using ordinary services or are inadequately served by them

- responses to new or newly discovered needs and problems

- work which is hard to finance through conventional fundraising

- one-off purchases or projects, including research

- short and medium-term work which is likely to bring a long-term benefit and/or to attract long-term funding from elsewhere.

Core funding is not ruled out for work which falls into one or more of these categories.

Because trusts vary enormously in their policies, styles of working and administrative capacities, there are three golden rules about applying for funding:

- do your homework beforehand

- prepare your application carefully

- leave plenty of time.

Selecting trusts

Use the various published directories and online resources to locate trusts which may be able to help – and to rule out those which will not be interested. Draw up a shortlist of possible trusts. Your list should include:

• trusts which operate in your geographical area. Look especially for any trusts which can only fund in your area or which express a preference for it. Don't approach a trust which cannot fund in your area, or ask for funding for a national project from a trust which is limited to a particular locality. A trust which funds nationally may be interested in a local project if it particularly matches the trust's interests and/or is of national significance; that is it would make a grant because of the pioneering nature of the project's work rather than because of the needs of the area. Only the very largest national trusts (the top 50 or so) are able to fund local projects more widely than this

• trusts which are interested in your field of work and the sort of people who will benefit from it. If a trust says that it makes grants only in a particular field or to benefit a particular age group, it means it. Likewise if a trust says that it does not fund general appeals or that projects of a particular type are excluded, don't try to persuade it that you are the exception

• trusts which make (and have sufficient funds to make) grants of the size you need. Don't ask a small trust for too much (or a large one for too little).

Many trusts publish information leaflets for applicants, and an increasing number have websites. Download or write off for these details and use them to refine your shortlist, which will usually be quite short – perhaps only three or four trusts, and probably not more than 20. Where a trust's information says that it has an application form, obtain this before proceeding; don't waste time drafting a letter until you have completed the form. Many trusts however do not use an application form.

If you can't find any trusts that seem likely to be interested, think again about how to present your work. Can you describe it in a different way, emphasising different (and preferably unusual) aspects that may attract a different group of funders? If the amount you need is too large, can you sub-divide the proposal into smaller projects?

Writing your application

There is likely to be an increasing trend for more outcomes focus. So ensure that you answer the questions 'What differences will you make?' and 'How will you know that you have actually made these differences?'.

Remember to include the following points:

• the purpose of the work to be funded – who it will help and how, what is distinctive about it, what will be achieved if a grant is given (and perhaps what will not be achieved if a grant is not given)

- a budget for the project. Work out your needs carefully. Don't economise on essentials such as training or unavoidable overhead costs

- ask for a specific sum. If necessary, say that you are seeking a contribution of £X towards a total budget of £Y, and that you hope to raise the remainder from other sources which you specify. Do not simply say that you are a very worthwhile organisation and desperately need funds

- your name, address, email address and phone number.

Make the application long enough to describe what you want properly, but short enough to be easy to take in at first reading – usually no more than two pages for your main letter. Don't overload the application with attachments. A trust which is seriously interested will ask for anything it doesn't have. However, you should always include your most recent annual report and accounts. (If your accounts show apparently large reserves, attach a note explaining why you hold them and why they cannot be used to fund the project for which you are seeking funds. If you cannot explain the size of your reserves, consider spending them instead of applying for grants!)

If your organisation does not have charitable status, explain why the work to be funded is charitable, and if possible name a registered charity that will take responsibility for any grant on your behalf (providing written confirmation from that charity). You *must* identify such a charity when applying to a trust that has a policy of only funding registered charities.

Connecting with trusts

Apply well before you need the money. Trusts generally make decisions through trustees' meetings which take place every two or three months. Some meet only two or three times a year. While a few trusts have small grants programmes where a fast response can be given, most are unable to deal quickly even with the very best applications.

Trusts generally have quite limited administrative capacity. Although the largest trusts are quite substantial organisations, only the top 300 or so employ any staff at all. The vast majority of trusts are run on a part-time or voluntary basis, and are themselves very small organisations. Don't expect too much of them. The sheer volume of applications means that most trusts do not normally acknowledge them, and many are unable to reply to applicants who are ultimately unsuccessful. If you want to be sure of an acknowledgement, send a self-addressed, reply-paid postcard.

Remember that trusts get many more applications than they can fund. A typical trust, if there is such a thing, may be able to fund only one in four of the eligible applications received, and half or more of the enquiries it receives may be ineligible because they are outside the trust's stated guidelines or lack obvious details such as a return address. If you don't succeed, it may not reflect on the quality of your application. It may just be that the trust has insufficient money to fund all the applications that it would like to support.

Visits

Some trusts will want to visit you, while others will deal with your application entirely by letter. Some will be willing to discuss the application (or a prospective application) over the phone, while others will not. (If a trust's directory entry does not include a phone number, this means that calls are unwelcome. It will not help you to trace the number.)

A visit is usually a sign that you have got over the first hurdle. Try to establish what the funder wishes to see and whom he or she wishes to meet. It is useful also to identify how long the funder can spend with you. Is the funder hoping to see your project in action as well as discuss the organisation's work? Is she or he interested in the whole organisation or just this particular project? The answers to these questions will help you decide who should be available to meet the funder at the visit.

Trusts usually make visits to assess the need for the project and the extent to which the applicants have come up with a good solution. They will also be looking for reassurance that the applicants have the ability to deliver what they promise. This is your chance to bring the project to life so try to ensure that the person meeting the funder both knows about the project and is enthusiastic about it.

A continuing relationship?

If you are lucky enough to receive an offer of a grant, ensure first of all that you acknowledge it and make arrangements to meet the conditions (if any) that are set for releasing payment. If you are simply sent a cheque, or when you receive it at a later stage, acknowledge and thank the funder – it is surprising how many applicants do not do this. Thereafter try to keep in touch in whatever way the funder suggests. If the funder wants frequent reports then make sure you supply them, but if the funder only wants a report once a year do not bombard it with information in between times.

Do let your funder know if there are problems. It is far better to be alerted at an early stage to any difficulties – when a funder may be able to help, for example, by varying the times at which the grant is paid, helping you identify other funders that might make up a shortfall, or offering advice if similar problems have occurred in other organisations. Don't wait until there is a real crisis before letting the funder know what is happening.

On the positive side, if you receive any particular significant good news – such as increased funding, good publicity or the achievement of a particular objective – do let your funders know. It is worth checking, perhaps six months before your current funding runs out, whether a particular funder is willing to consider a further application. Finally, please note that most members of the ACF can only fund registered charities.

Future trends

Because of fraud concerns it seems likely that applicants will find themselves having to provide more proof of identity than may have been the case in the past.

A note on terminology

The words 'trust' and 'foundation' are virtually synonymous. All charitable foundations are trusts, i.e. they are managed by trustees, who may or may not be supported by paid staff. A 'foundation' is a trust whose income derives from an endowment of land or invested capital. Not all foundations make grants; some use their income to finance charitable work of their own.

How do trusts spend their money?

The following information about trusts' interests is based on an analysis of 2,273 grants.

Main subject areas	Proportion of grants	Proportion of total grant expenditure	Main types of support given
Social care	36%	25%	Core/project
Health	11%	19%	Capital
Education	13%	17%	Core/project
Arts/culture/recreation	12%	10%	Project
Religious activities	9%	8%	Capital
Development/housing	5%	5%	Project
Environment/animals	3%	3%	Project
Philanthropy/volunteering	2%	3%	Core
Science and technology	1%	3%	Research
Civil society/law and advocacy	3%	3%	Core
International	2%	2%	Project/research
Social science	1%	2%	Research

Information from: *Patterns of Independent Grantmaking in the UK*, 2000 published by CAF

CHAPTER FOURTEEN

Foundations in the US: securing grants for British causes

David Wickert

Overview

There are many similarities between UK grant-making trusts and US foundations. This chapter focuses on US non-profit grant-making organisations, usually called foundations. It highlights similarities and explains the significance of the differences by outlining how US foundations operate. It does not deal with the full range of American fundraising opportunities offered by individual American taxpayers, companies, US expatriates and others with US taxed income worldwide.

Why should a foundation fund in the UK?

Here are some reasons:

● Links of language, history and culture give added value and make the UK a particularly attractive choice for American grantmaking.

● Personal contact. If your supporters, trustees, volunteers or clients include American members of a board of a US foundation this may provide the personal introduction that fundraisers value above almost everything.

● An overlap of interests. A US company in the UK sees a chance to enhance its profile in your community, where it has customers, suppliers and employees, by supporting your organisation.

● Your charity works in a third country, work not done there by any US non-profit or complementary to the work of a US non-profit.

● Your charity needs funding for innovative research. The research is important in the US and your research identifies funding for the work there.

● You are planning to tour, exhibit or work regularly with a US non-profit organisation.

● You have alumni or members in the US.

US foundations: who gives, who receives and how much?

Like UK grant-making trusts, most US foundations were established to support a particular community or local cause.

In 2007 US foundations made grants in excess of $40 billion, including grants to support causes outside the US that totalled nearly $4.5 billion. However, set against the total giving from all sources in 2007 – $306.39 billion – the amount given outside the US is modest.

Out of a total of 104,813 grant-making foundations reviewed for this article, 17,156 (16%) have been involved in some way with international grantmaking, although, of course not necessarily to the UK.

The names of some of the international grantmakers are very well known and they provide detailed information for applicants outside the US, for example Gates, Mott, Ford, Rockefeller, Getty and Amex. The Global Fund for Women, the Ford Foundation, the Rockefeller Foundation and others, make a majority of their grants outside the US. There are a few foundations that *only* make grants outside the US, for example the Christopher Reynolds Foundation, the China Medical Board and the Central European University Foundation.

Other foundations don't advertise the fact that they fund outside the US. But information about every US non-profit organisation, including foundations, can be found from their Form 990 tax returns which are publicly available at www.guidestar.org.

The structure of American philanthropy

The philanthropic sector in the US is, very broadly, divided into two: public charities and private foundations (including foundations set up by individuals and company foundations). These two categories are similar to operating charities and grant-making trusts in the UK. In both cases the first group offers services and the second group makes grants to fund the services offered. However, the laws that regulate them in the US are very different from charity law in the UK.

In the US, Section 501(c)(3) is a part of the US Internal Revenue Code that designates tax exempt organisations. Both public charities and private foundations qualify under Section 501(c)(3). 501(c)(3) is a technical term that you will find in application guidelines. In this chapter we have called public charities 'non-profits'. Private foundations we have called 'foundations'.

US non-profits are funded by donations from the public and by grants from foundations. Foundations are funded by an individual, a small group of individuals, a family or a company. The funder often provides an endowment.

To understand how foundations operate it is necessary to know the major differences between the UK and the US tax systems as they relate to charitable giving.

In the US there is no tax reclaim, or Gift Aid. In the US there is a *tax deduction*.

When a US individual or company makes a donation to a non-profit or a foundation their taxable income is reduced by the amount they give. Because the donation reduces the amount of income tax they pay, a deduction is perceived as a benefit to a donor. And the non-profit gets the total value of the donation directly from the donor. This is unlike the UK where the charity gets the donation minus tax, and the tax reclaimed is regarded as a benefit to the charity that reclaims it.

It is straightforward for a US individual or company to get a tax deduction. It involves retaining the receipt for the donation provided by the non-profit and entering details of the gift on an annual tax return.

Importantly for the purposes of this chapter, no deduction can be taken for a gift made to a charity outside the US. There is no law against US donors sending cheques directly to charitable organisations in the UK, but the absence of a tax deduction does, effectively, make large donations unusual.

Although 17% of American foundations make grants directly to charitable organisations outside the US, these foundations are responsible for significant due diligence to ensure that the non-US organisations qualify as suitable recipients under US law. There are penalties if they get this wrong. This deters foundations from giving outside the US.

'Friends'

There are ways for charities outside the US to make it easier for foundations to provide them with funding.

The first is for the non-US charity to set up a public charity which can support it. These public charities often (but certainly not always) include the word 'friends' in their name, for example: University College London Friends and Alumni Association, Inc. In this chapter we describe these nonprofits as 'Friends' even though this is not necessarily part of their name. For example, the American Friends organisation of the National Trust is called the Royal Oak Foundation.

Friends are independent American organisations controlled by a board of directors who are governed by US federal and state law. Friends are not a subsidiary of the organisation that arranged for them to be set up.

US taxpayers can take a tax deduction for a donation to a Friends organisation. And because it's independent, the Friends organisation isn't obliged to support any particular organisation, and money raised by the

Friends isn't automatically transferred to a charity outside the US. Grants are made by a Friends organisation following a decision of the board: the board may require a grant application, it will undertake suitable due diligence, and a board's decision will be recorded in the minutes of the meeting.

However, a Friends organisation may invite, welcome, consider and follow suggestions from donors regarding recipients of the grants that it makes.

There is an alternative to American Friends. There are US non-profits that, as a part of their mission, fund charitable organisations outside the US. They do the necessary due diligence on the non-US organisations, and invite US foundations and individual taxpayers to make donations to them and suggest non-US charities to receive grants from them. US non-profits that work like this include the American Fund for Charities www.american fund.info and the Charities Aid Foundation America www.cafamerica.org.

Other UK charities have developed close reciprocal links with a US non-profit, often one doing similar work. This US non-profit will accept grants from a foundation or individual. If a non-US charity is suggested as a grantee, and after board consideration, the board can make a grant.

Without a Friends organisation, or with a supportive intermediary non-profit, many US foundations will not fund a charitable organisation outside the US. And individual US supporters can't get a tax deduction for a donation to support your organisation.

Finding the right foundation to fund you

The last ten years have seen a complete revolution in US foundation research. Ten years ago it was hard copy directory based; now it's on the internet.

Ideally, you need a fully searchable database of US foundations that will disclose as much information about each foundation as available. Information should include:

- contact details

- directors and key staff

- website address

- what the foundation says it supports and where

- what it has actually supported and where

- a breakdown of how much it gives annually and to what and where

- how to make an application

- when to apply

- when grants are made

- whether a preliminary application is required

- details of what information to include in a full application

- how long before you have an answer

- whether you are welcome to contact or visit the foundation to meet staff and ask questions

- if you receive – or don't receive – a grant how long before you can apply again.

Searchable databases that provide this information include the Foundation Center Directory Online www.foundationcenter.org and Foundation Search www.foundationsearch.com, which is managed by a Canadian organisation and is particularly aware of the requirements of fundraisers outside the US.

Foundations that indicate that they do not accept unsolicited applications don't necessarily mean that they don't accept unsolicited applications! It may mean that they only accept a preliminary application (often called a Letter of Inquiry in the US, a two or three-page summary of an application) and don't accept full applications unsolicited. Look at the guidelines carefully. If in doubt, ask the foundation.

Under no circumstances send one mass-produced appeal to every foundation you can think of whether or not you have their guidelines.

Preparing your application

Prepare your application by providing the foundation with exactly what the guidelines ask for, neither more nor less. If there is something that you cannot provide you must say why. Translate figures into dollars. Add international dialling codes to telephone and fax numbers; in fact do everything and anything to make the application as easy to understand as possible.

It is at this point that assistance from a real live American can be invaluable, although only someone with experience of non-profits will be able to translate the technical language that may come up. Ask this American to read your completed application to identify if there are any words or phrases that will be incomprehensible in the US, or mean something completely different. For example, 'scheme' means 'scam' to an American – remember the UK English connection between 'scheme' and disreputable 'scheming'; fortnights are two weeks and Esq means a lawyer and not a gentleman.

One thing that the guidelines will not tell you is how much to apply for. This is obviously a very significant decision, and you should ask for a grant that is reasonable to expect from the organisation you are applying to, taking into account its financial resources and the size of grants it usually makes to organisations such as yours. You will usually be asked what grants have already been received, what has been promised and what has been applied for, in the US and the UK and elsewhere.

Many foundations accept applications by email, but follow their instructions. Some foundations will acknowledge applications, others will not. Some will only contact you if your application is successful. If you are successful thank them, and ask if they know other foundations which might consider funding your projects. The foundation world is a small world when it comes to such matters. Be sure to fulfil to the letter all the reporting requirements regarding your use of the grant.

If you are unsuccessful, telephone and ask (nicely!) why the foundation didn't fund you (presuming that it has not told you in enough detail in the rejection letter), and ask if it knows of any other foundation that might consider funding your project. It may think your project is great but just did not have the funding available.

Conclusion

I once met a fundraiser who said he started telephoning US foundations and within half an hour had a firm commitment and two days later a cheque for a vast sum was hand-delivered!

If this hasn't happened why not try it?

But just in case it doesn't work, follow the advice in this chapter and start seriously researching appropriate funders and preparing some well thought through applications.

CHAPTER FIFTEEN

DSC's Great Giving campaign

Jay Kennedy

Over the years DSC has campaigned on a number of fronts for better grant-making. We believe that funders have a responsibility that extends far beyond providing money. The way funders operate and develop their programmes has a huge impact on the organisations, causes and beneficiaries which their funding supports, as well as the wider voluntary sector.

Transparency is a key principle for us; by providing information about funders in DSC publications we have sought to open up their practices to greater scrutiny. Clearer and more accessible information enables fundraisers to focus their efforts effectively, and encourages open review and discussions of good practice.

Our Great Giving campaign has grown out of these long-established beliefs and the experience of our research. It includes some specific areas that we want to focus on as part of an overall campaign for better grant-making.

A clear picture of the funding environment

More comprehensive information about where money is going and what it is supporting is needed, to enable better planning and decision-making by funders and policymakers. In our first *Funders' Almanac* we analysed data we already held on funders in a more strategic way, as a step towards providing a 'clearer picture'.

Accessible funding for campaigning

Financial support for campaigning is vital to the role organisations play in achieving social change. We are working to provide greater clarity about which grant-making trusts fund campaigning activity, so that campaigning organisations can more easily find support.

An end to hidden small print

The terms and conditions of funding agreements can compromise the independence of funded organisations, partly because they are not sufficiently transparent. We are asking all funders to make any information which governs the use of the funds available when people apply, and to be open to negotiating terms when applicants request it.

No ineligible applications

Most funders receive applications that do not fall within their guidelines – ineligible applications. DSC research shows that over one third of applications to trusts and foundations are ineligible, and for government funding the figure is closer to half. Clearer guidelines and feedback can help, but applicants also need to take more heed of funder guidelines and target applications appropriately.

For more on DSC's Great Giving campaign, go to www.dsc.org.uk/greatgiving.

References

Funders' Almanac, Jay Kennedy, Amy Rosser, Tom Traynor and Ben Wittenberg, DSC, 2008

Critical Conditions: Investigating the transparency of grant terms and conditions, Jay Kennedy, DSC, 2010

Ineligible Applications, DSC, 2010

In conclusion

Anthony Clay

Introduction

Since editing the first edition of this book in 1997 we have seen many changes, from the introduction of the Charities Act 2006 to the widespread arrival of the internet as a key fundraising tool, to the worst recession for some 60 years.

Some would say that in spite of all this, the grant-making trust scene has remained relatively constant. For example, the reaction of the major grantmakers to the sudden arrival of the credit crisis in 2008 was to say that they did not expect major upheaval. They tend to plan their grant programmes several years ahead. The major concern was what would happen when the country finally faced up to the huge cuts in government expenditure that seemed inevitable. At the time of writing, these cuts have barely begun to happen and in the meantime the portfolios of many grantmakers have been restored to 2008 levels because of the recovery of world stock markets between early 2009 and early 2010.

Although the overall picture may not have been one of dramatic change, there is, in fact, considerable movement in the fortunes and activities of trusts – see Chapter 3 for more on this. From time to time new trusts emerge, through either mergers (e.g. Lloyds TSB Foundation), events (e.g. the Diana, Princess of Wales Memorial Fund) or government initiatives (e.g. the Big Lottery Fund). Although, mercifully, we have not recently seen many trusts shrinking dramatically (e.g. the Baring Foundation in 1994) there have been some major shocks, such as the disappearance of the Camelot Foundation and the Laidlaw Youth Trust. There have also been remarkable increases in a some trusts' ability to make grants. For example, when in 1999 the Esmée Fairbairn Foundation sold its holding in M&G as part of that company's takeover by Prudential Corporation plc, the Foundation's endowment grew significantly in value – and so did the size and scope of the grants it was able to make. Also the Garfield Weston Foundation has steadily increased its grant-making capacity as a result of the profitability and increased dividend payments of its parent company, Associated British Foods.

How will grantmaker react to such changes?

The dramatic growth in information about grantmakers on the internet, from the trusts' own websites, from new and established fundraising research companies and media (such as the annual *Sunday Times Rich List*) may result in continuing increases in applications, as may increasing professionalism in charities that had not previously taken trust fundraising very seriously.

All these pressures will be making grantmakers think hard about how they process enquiries and indeed, in some cases, whether they can process them at all. Some may, therefore, look nervously at the arrival of the latest edition of this book, for fear that it may have the effect of stimulating more and more pressure. It is to be hoped that this will not be the case.

Time and again the authors of these pages have been urging research and focus, so that fewer trusts will be approached for irrelevant causes and that applications will be more relevant to the grantmakers' objects and policies. After all, trust administrators have been as likely to complain of a shortage of good projects for funding as of there being too many.

The responsibilities of grantseekers

Grantseekers have a duty to do their homework and get to know the grantmakers and what they are looking for. In turn the grantmakers are becoming increasingly proactive, in some cases even creating their own projects for funding and asking very searching questions of the charities they fund.

It is increasingly likely that charities seeking grants will be rejected until they satisfy the grantmakers that they have done all they can to secure the support of local people, are making maximum use of volunteers, have very well prepared fundraising strategies and have addressed the key issues as stated on the grantmakers' websites.

As times change so, doubtless, will the tasks of grantmaker and grant-seeker. Major new, and sometimes unexpected, influences will make important differences. We can be rightly apprehensive about stock market crashes, the effects of inflation, deflation, new world disasters. But, as is revealed in the most recent issue of *The Sunday Times Rich List,* we can be equally optimistic about the arrival on the scene of new super rich phil-anthropists, a growing awareness by major companies of the importance of being seen to be providing practical benefits to the community, and of trusts developing new and creative ways of helping good causes with their revenue as well as with their capital funding needs.

Looking to the future

To make predictions is to risk becoming a hostage to fortune, but there are some future directions that may be tentatively outlined, based on current trends.

The biggest single change will almost certainly come as a result of the dramatic cuts in public spending which, at the time of writing, are about to hit us. These are likely to be big and dramatic, placing tremendous new pressures on grantmakers, with consequent effects on their priorities and funding.

As ACF has pointed out in Chapter 13, it is clear that grantmakers are looking more and more at outcomes. 'What difference will you make with this grant?' is increasingly the question they are asking.

There will be an increasing trend towards applicants having to be clear about their carbon footprints and response to climate change, whatever the nature of their work.

The public benefit requirements will increasingly impact on applications and grantmakers will be required to be clear about this. Grantseekers, in turn, will increasingly have to make public benefit statements in applications.

Trusts will continue to become more active in seeking out projects in which they are interested. Some of them may continue a recent trend to become fundraisers themselves to increase their ability to make grants. This is epitomised by the community foundation movement (see page 10), which has grown much in recent years.

Perhaps the biggest change in the future will be the increasing role of partnership, in the way trusts see themselves working with charity, where the grantseeker is no longer a mere applicant but just as much an accomplice with the grantmaker.

With regard to what trusts will be seeking to fund in the years ahead, things are perhaps unlikely to change a great deal. Trusts will quite often change their policies, but things tend to be cyclical and, as new ideas become old ideas, so old ideas come round again as new ones.

Many grantmakers are most fearful of finding themselves 'on a hook', so to speak, when the charities they support become too dependent on them. There will always be efforts to wean these charities away from their grantmakers.

Grantmakers will continue to favour 'pump-priming' projects which set examples to others. Increasingly, they will be looking for serious evaluation of the success or otherwise of projects they have funded.

As a final conclusion, there are four key things for you to bear in mind:

• Trusts exist to give money away – if you can prove relevance, they should be truly glad to hear from you.

• Try to ensure that your application is clear and is what the grantmaker is looking for.

• Try to arrange things so that your first communication with a trust reaches it through some route other than the post-box – for example, a personal visit, the telephone, a fax or even an email.

• Follow the 10 golden rules listed below, especially the last one.

Trusts, like people, do not respond best to requests from institutions, projects, causes or charities. They are happier with requests from people whom they like and respect and who understand their needs.

---

10 golden rules for approaching trusts

1 Know your charity.
2 Know your trusts.
3 Match your charity to your trusts.
4 Be as personal as possible.
5 Do not send blanket mailshots.
6 Be brief, clear and frank.
7 Avoid jargon, hyperbole, tired words and phrases.
8 Use affirmation – not just assertion.
9 Invest adequately in time and resources.
10 Remember that 'people give to people'.

Sources of further help

Publications

Directory of Social Change: biennial directories

The Directory of Grant Making Trusts

Provides details of approximately 2,500 grant-making trusts.

The Guide to Educational Grants

Provides a detailed listing of educational charities and other sources of educational grants.

The Guide to Grants for Individuals in Need

Provides information on charities, welfare funds and benevolent funds that give financial support to individuals.

The Guide to the Major Trusts – volumes 1 and 2

Volume 1 concentrates on the 400 largest trusts that give over £300,000 a year, with a combined grantmaking total of around £2.53 billion. Volume 2 examines a further 1,100 mainly smaller trusts, which between them give around £212 million.

The Guide to New Trusts

Features in detail around 100 newly registered grant-making trusts.

The Guide to UK Company Giving

Details around 600 companies that support voluntary and community activities.

Directory of Social Change: specialist funding guides

These include the *Youth Funding Guide*, *Sports Funding Guide*, *Environment Funding Guide* and *Government Funding Guide*.

To order any of these titles or to see our full publications list visit DSC's website: www.dsc.org.uk or telephone 08450 77 77 07.

Other sources

Debrett's People of Today

A guide to Britain's meritocracy and a biographical study of the UK's most influential and successful people, recognising the achievements of over 25,000 people drawn from every sector of society.

Published by Debrett's Limited, 18–20 Hill Rise, Richmond, Surrey, TW10 6UA; tel: 020 8939 2250; website: www.debretts.com.

European Union Grants Directory

Contains outline details of grants available from the EU. Subscription includes an update service. Published by the EU Money Service, 40 Millias Close, Brough, HU15 1GP UK; email: info@europeangrants.com; website: www.europeangrants.com; tel: 01482 651695.

Websites

Directory of Social Change

Companygiving.org.uk

A subscription-based online directory that details around 600 companies that give cash donations and other forms of community support: www.company giving.org.uk.

Governmentfunding.org.uk

A subscription website containing over £2.3 billion in local, regional, national and European funding: www.governmentfunding.org.uk.

Grantsforindividuals.org.uk

A subscription-based online database of data from the print-based publications *The Guide to Grants for Individuals in Need* and *The Guide to Educational Grants*: www.grantsforindividuals.org.uk.

Trustfunding.org.uk

A subscription-based online directory of over 4,300 grant-making trusts.

To subscribe go to the relevant website address (or follow the links on www.dsc.org.uk), or telephone 08450 77 77 07.

dsc.org.uk/greatgiving

Free information and reports about DSC's Great Giving campaign to improve funding for charities and voluntary groups. website: www.dsc.org. uk/greatgiving.

Other sources

fit4funding

Previously Charities Information Bureau, this website provides online help and advice for community groups and voluntary organisations who are seeking funding. fit4funding also publishes a subscription-based monthly e-newsletter on funding.

fit4funding, The Charities Information Bureau, 93 Lawefield Lane, Wakefield, WF2 8SU; email: info@fit4funding.org.uk; website: fit4funding. org.uk; tel: 01924 239063

fundinginformation.org

Provides subscription-based information on sources of funding opportunities for the voluntary sector. Inspiring Vision LLP, 77 Bunwell Street, Bunwell, Norfolk, NR16 1AB; email: info@inspiring-vision.com; website: www.fundinginformation.org; tel: 01953789816.

Funding Central

A free website for charities, voluntary organisations and social enterprises. The site provides access to 4,000 funding and finance opportunities, plus tools and resources to help organisations develop sustainable income strategies appropriate to their needs. c/o NCVO, Regent's Wharf, 8 All Saints Street, London, N1 9RL, email: fundingcentral@ncvo-vol.org.uk; website: www.fundingcentral.org.uk; tel: 020 7520 2523

Useful addresses

Charity commissions

The Charity Commission for England and Wales
Charity Commission Direct, PO Box 1227, Liverpool, L69 3UG
Email: send via website form
Website: www.charity-commission.gov.uk
Tel: 0845 300 0218

Office of the Scottish Charity Regulator (OSCR)
2nd Floor, Quadrant House, 9 Riverside Drive, Dundee, DD1 4NY
Email: info@oscr.org.uk
Website: www.oscr.org.uk
Tel: 01382 220446

Charity Commission for Northern Ireland (CCNI)
4th Floor, 24–26 Arthur Street, Belfast, BT1 4GF
Email: admin@charitycommissionni.org.uk
Website: www.charitycommissionni.org.uk
Tel: 028 9051 5490

Each Commission's website contains an online register of charities for the respective areas. Note that the commissions prefer to receive correspondence via email rather than by post.

Other useful addresses

The American Fund for Charities
c/o Chapel & York Ltd
1000 North West Street, Suite 1200, Wilmington, DE 19801, USA
Email: contact@americanfund.info
Website: www.chapel-york.com
Tel: (+1) 302 295 4959

Association of Charitable Foundations
ACF's website includes downloadable copies of advice leaflets, facts and figures about trusts and foundations, links to trust and foundation websites, UK and international umbrella bodies, and other useful resources for grantseekers.
Central House, 14 Upper Woburn Place, London, WC1H 0AE
Email: acf@acf.org.uk
Website: www.acf.org.uk
Tel: 020 7255 4499

Chapel & York
A company that specialises in helping UK charities to seek grants from the USA.
12 The Courtyard, Ladycross Business Park, Hollow Lane, Lingfield, RH7 6PB
Email: info@chapel-york.com
Website: www.chapel-york.com
Tel: 01342 871910

Charities Aid Foundation (CAF)

The Charities Aid Foundation works to create greater value for charities and social enterprise by transforming the way donations are made and the way charitable funds are managed.
Head office, Kings Hill House, 25 Kings Hill, West Malling, ME19 4TA
Email: enquiries@cafonline.org
Website: www.cafonline.org
Tel: 03000 123 000

Charities Aid Foundation America

King Street Station, Suite 150, 1800 Diagonal Road, Alexandria, VA 22314–2840, USA
Email: info@cafamerica.org
Website: www.cafamerica.org
Tel: (+1) 703 549 8931

Community Foundation Network

Umbrella organisation for UK community trusts and foundations.
12 Angel Gate, 320–326 City Road, London, EC1V 2PT
Email: network@communityfoundations.org.uk
Website: www.communityfoundations.org.uk
Tel: 020 7713 9326

Directory of Social Change

See 'About the Directory of Social Change' on page 129

European Foundation

Provides comment and analysis on European integration.
83 Victoria Street, London, SW1H OHW
Email: vasconcelos@e-f.org.uk
Website: www.europeanfoundation.org
Tel: 020 3178 7038

The European Foundation Centre

An international association of foundations and corporate funders. The website contains some resources and advice for grantseekers.
European Foundation Centre, AISBL, 78, avenue de la Toison d'Or, 1060 Brussels, Belgium
Email: efc@efc.be
Tel: +32 2512 8938
Website: www.efc.be

Factary
Provides a research service for not-for-profit organisations and publishes the monthly *New Trust Update*.
Brunswick Court, Brunswick Square, Bristol, BS2 8PE
Email: nicolaw@factary.com
Website: www.factary.com
Tel: 0117 9166 740

The Foundation Center
Provides information on US grantmakers and their funding activities.
79 Fifth Avenue, New York, NY 10003–3076, USA
Email: via the online form
Website: www. foundationcenter.org
Tel: (+1) 212 6204 230

The Funding Network
An organisation that brings individual donors together to identify and support projects.
16 Lincoln's Inn Fields, London, WC2A 3ED
Email: info@thefundingnetwork.org.uk
Website: www.thefundingnetwork.org.uk
Tel: 0845 313 8449

Institute of Fundraising
The professional body for not-for-profit fundraisers in the UK.
Park Place, 12 Lawn Lane, London, SW8 1UD
Email: via the online form
Website: www.institute-of-fundraising.org.uk
Tel: 020 7840 1000

National Council for Voluntary Organisations (NCVO)
Provides information, advice and support for those working in and for the voluntary sector in England.
Regent's Wharf, 8 All Saints Street, London, N1 9RL
Email: ncvo@ncvo-vol.org.uk
Website: www.ncvo-vol.org.uk
Tel: 020 7713 6161

NAVCA
NAVCA is the national voice of local support and development organisations in England.
The Tower, 2 Furnival Square, Sheffield, S1 4QL
Email: navca@navca.org.uk

Website: www.navca.org.uk
Tel: 0114 278 6636

New Philanthropy Capital
A consultancy and think tank dedicated to helping funders and charities achieve a greater impact. Offers advice based on in-depth research of social issues.
3 Downstream, 1 London Bridge, London, SE1 9BG
Email: info@philanthropycapital.org
Website: www.philanthropycapital.org
Tel: 020 7785 6300

Northern Ireland Council for Voluntary Action (NICVA)
The national body representing the voluntary sector in Northern Ireland.
61 Duncairn Gardens, Belfast, BT15 2GB
Email: info@nicva.org
Website: www.nicva.org
Tel: 028 9087 7777

The Projects Company
Provides accredited training in project management and fundraising.
Willow Lodge, Church Road, High Beach, Loughton, IG10 4AJ
Email: info@theprojectsco.co.uk
Website: www.theprojectsco.co.uk
Tel: 020 8502 2327

Scottish Council for Voluntary Organisations (SCVO)
The national body representing the voluntary sector in Scotland.
Mansfield Traquair Centre, 15 Mansfield Place, Edinburgh, EH3 6BB
Email: enquiries@scvo.org.uk
Website: www.scvo.org.uk
Tel: 0131 556 3882

Welsh Council for Voluntary Action (WCVA)
The national body representing the voluntary sector in Wales.
Baltic House, Mount Stuart Square, Cardiff Bay Cardiff, CF10 5FH
Email: help@wcva.org.uk
Website: www.wcva.org.uk
Tel: 0800 2888 329

Institute of Fundraising Codes of Fundraising Practice and Code of Conduct

The Institute of Fundraising's Codes of Fundraising Practice set out the best practice standards for fundraisers operating within the UK. Each Code covers a separate fundraising technique or issue, as well as an overarching Code of Conduct setting out the framework of ethical behaviour for fundraisers. The Codes provide not only information on relevant areas of the law but outline recommended practice based upon the highest standards of fundraising. A new feature is a checklist on the front of each Code making them even more accessible to fundraisers.

All 5,000+ Individual and 300+ Organisational members of the Institute have already committed to meet the best practice guidance outlined within the Codes. The Codes are the best practice criteria upon which the self-regulatory scheme for fundraising is built.

The Codes are drawn up by working parties composed of representatives of the various interested constituents in a particular field, and undergo an extensive public consultation process, which includes charities affiliated with the Institute of Fundraising, regulators and Government. As new areas of interest are identified, so new Codes are drafted, under the supervision of the Institute of Fundraising Standards Committee.

Codes of Fundraising Practice

Acceptance and Refusal of Donations
Accountability and Transparency
Best Practice for Fundraising Consultants
Best Practice for Fundraising Contracts
Best Practice for Major Donor Fundraising
Charities Working with Business
Charity Challenge Events
Committed Giving in the Workplace
Data Protection
Direct Mail
Event Fundraising
Face-to-Face Fundraising (on the street and house-to-house)

Fundraising from Grant Making Trusts
Fundraising in Schools
Fundraising through Electronic Media
Handling of Cash Donations
House-to-House Collections
Legacy Fundraising
Outdoor Fundraising in the UK
Payment of Fundraisers
Raffles and Lotteries
Reciprocal Charity Mailing
Telephone Fundraising
Telephone Recruitment of Collectors
The Management of Static Collection Boxes
Use of Chain Letters as a Fundraising Technique
Volunteer Fundraising

Guidance

Guidance for 'In Aid Of' Volunteer Fundraisers
Model Contracts and Standard Forms of Agreement

New Codes for 2011

Being Revised:
House to House Collections – currently out for public consultation
Handling of Cash Donations
Fundraising through Electronic Media

Copies of the Codes of Practice and Code of Conduct including the Fundraising from Grant Making Trusts code of practice can be downloaded from the Institute of Fundraising's website: www.institute-of-fundraising.org.uk

For further information please contact the Policy Team at:

Institute of Fundraising
Park Place
12 Lawn Lane
London
SW8 1UD
Tel: 020 7840 1028
Fax: 020 7840 1001
Email: codes@institute-of-fundraising.org.uk

APPENDIX THREE

Glossary

501(c)3 US-designated charity, from a section of the Internal Revenue Service Code of the US

Accountability The responsibility of a grant-receiving organisation to keep the grant makers informed about the use of the grant.

Acknowledge To express gratitude for (a grant) in written or oral form, communicated privately or publicly.

Action grant A grant awarded to support an operating programme or project (also see Research grant).

Administrator The person who administers a grant-making trust.

Advocate To speak or write in favour of a cause, or a person who advocates.

Allocations committee A group responsible for grant-making decisions.

Annual report A yearly report of the financial and overall state of an organisation.

Anonymous gift A gift that is not publicly attributed to the donor.

Appeal letter A letter requesting a donation to a fundraising campaign.

Area of interest A grantmaker's interest in a particular cause.

Benefactor A donor.

Beneficiary Someone, or an organisation, receiving a grant from a generous donor.

Bricks/mortar campaign Capital fundraising to meet the financial needs for constructing a building, including fixtures and fittings.

Business plan Specific steps and timetable required to accomplish an organisational objective.

Campaign (fundraising) An organised effort to raise a specified amount of money for a particular purpose in a specified period.

Campaign analysis A report on the results and effectiveness of a fundraising campaign.

Capital campaign An intensive fundraising effort to meet a specific financial goal within a specified period that is out of the ordinary and not for revenue purposes. Usually for buildings, property, equipment or an endowment.

Capital expenditure The amount needed to acquire an asset having an expected useful life of more than one year.

Case The reason why an organisation both merits and needs philanthropic support.

Case statement A presentation that sets out a case.

Cash flow Funds that are available within a given time.

Charitable Incorporated Organisation (CIO) A new corporate structure designed specifically for charities which can offer several benefits over unincorporated structures. These benefits include: the members and trustees are usually personally safeguarded from the financial liabilities the charity incurs, which is not normally the case for unincorporated charities; the charity has a legal personality of its own, enabling it to conduct business in its own name, rather than the name of its trustees.

Charitable trust A trust established to benefit one or more charities.

Charity The Charities Act 2006 (which applies to England and Wales. Scotland and Northern Ireland have their own legislation) – the latest legislation in this field – states that a charity is an organisation whose purpose is one which falls within certain descriptions set out in Section 2 of the Act: see 'Charity status', page 12.

Demonstration grant An initial grant given to develop or launch a programme or project that may function as a model.

Endowment A permanently restricted net asset, the principal of which is protected and the income from which may be spent on a specific purpose.

Foundation Technically a trust whose income derives from an endowment of money or invested capital. In effect synonymous with a 'trust'.

Gift-range table A projection of the number of gifts needed, by size, to achieve a particular fundraising goal.

Lead gift A gift donated at the beginning of a campaign that is expected to set a standard for future giving.

Major gift A significant donation, the amount required to qualify as a major gift being determined by the fundraising organisation (usually more than £5,000).

New money A gift of money that exceeds a donor's gift the previous year, a gift from a newly acquired donor, a large amount of money recently acquired by a person or family, or self-made rather than inherited wealth.

Old money Wealth inherited by one generation from another.

Outcomes The results and consequences, presumably beneficial, of a project or programme of work funded by a grant-making trust.

Overheads General expenses that are necessary to an organisation.

Philanthropy The promotion of human beings' welfare, especially through acts or gifts (often financial) done or given to good causes.

Pledge A promise that is written, signed and dated, to fulfil a commitment at some future time.

Principal A sum of money on which interest is paid.

Prospect Any potential donor whose relationship to the charity, interests and giving ability have been confirmed.

Research grant A grant awarded for scientific or marketing research work. (also see Action grant)

Strategic plan Decisions and action that shape and guide an organisation while emphasising the future implications of present decisions.

Trust An arrangement establishing a judiciary relationship in which a trustor conveys property to a trustee to hold and manage for the benefit of one or more beneficiaries.

Trustee A person or institution holding the legal title to property in a trust and having responsibility for managing it, often a member of a governing board.

Trustor A person making a gift to set up a trust.

Unrestricted gift or grant A gift made without any conditions or designation.

Verbal pledge An oral promise to make a gift or grant.

Working capital Money available to pay current operating expenses.

About the Directory of Social Change

The Directory of Social Change (DSC) has a vision of a better society through independent voluntary action. We believe that society can be changed for the better when citizens take responsibility for themselves, their communities and each other.

The activities of independent charities, voluntary organisations and community groups are fundamental to achieve social change. We exist to help these organisations and the people who support them to achieve their goals.

We do this by:

• providing practical tools that organisations and activists need, including online and printed publications, training courses, and conferences on a huge range of topics
• acting as a 'concerned citizen' in public policy debates, often on behalf of smaller charities, voluntary organisations and community groups
• leading campaigns and stimulating debate on key policy issues that affect those groups
• carrying out research and providing information to influence policymakers.

DSC is the leading provider of information and training for the voluntary sector and publishes an extensive range of guides and handbooks covering subjects such as fundraising, management, communication, finance and law. We have a range of subscription-based websites containing a wealth of information on funding from trusts, companies and government sources. We run more than 300 training courses each year, including bespoke in-house training provided at the client's location. DSC conferences, many of which run on an annual basis, include the Charity Management Conference, the Charity Accountants' Conference and the Charity Law Conference. DSC's major annual event is Charityfair, which provides low-cost training on a wide variety of subjects.

For details of all our activities, and to order publications and book courses, go to www.dsc.org.uk, call 08450 777707 or email publications@dsc.org.uk

About the Institute of Fundraising

As the UK's professional body, the Institute of Fundraising (IoF) supports more than 5,000 individual fundraisers and 300 charities. Formed more than 25 years ago by a group of fundraisers getting together to share and tackle fundraising issues, a lot has changed since then. However, this 'brief' remains at the heart of what the IoF is all about, i.e. supporting fundraisers in the challenges they meet as individuals and as part of the sector.

Fundraisers have a tough job – a rewarding one, but a tough one all the same. The IoF helps to make that job a little easier by providing support such as training leading to professional qualifications, offering sound guidance and advice and helping fundraisers to become part of a large and vibrant fundraising network.

Members join because they are committed to achieving the highest standards in fundraising and have confidence in the Institute to help them do that. They agree to abide by a set of Codes of Conduct and Codes of Fundraising Practice which form the basis of self-regulation for the profession and they are committed to developing their career. The IoF is committed to promoting fundraising as a profession – and giving it the credibility and recognition that it deserves – and is currently developing a framework of qualifications which will meet the needs of fundraisers at every stage of their careers.

The IoF offers an extensive programme of training and development events. The flagship event, IoF National Convention, is the largest fundraising event of its type outside the USA, attracting around 2,000 charity representatives of all levels: CEOs, fundraisers, marketing and communication professionals and policy advisers. This three-day programme is supplemented by a series of targeted/subject-specific one-day fundraising conferences taking place throughout the year.

The Institute is represented across the UK by a range of national, regional and special interest groups. National and regional groups support fundraisers locally through events, training, networking and peer support. Special interest groups offer technique specific support to fundraisers, providing a forum for the exchange of ideas and best practice as well as excellent networking opportunities. Through IoF's campaigning work – such as fighting for improvements to Gift Aid or contesting the Payment's Council's proposals to abolish cheques, with the devastating impact that could have on charitable donations – the Institute is here to represent and support its members.

Index